Neil Root and Ia

WHO KILLED ROSEMARY NELSON?

At last, the full story of the conspiracy
behind the assassination of Northern Ireland's
top human rights lawyer.

JOHN BLAKE

364/1524.

Published by John Blake Publishing Ltd,
3 Bramber Court, 2 Bramber Road,
London W14 9PB, England

www.johnblakepublishing.co.uk

www.facebook.com/Johnblakepub facebook
twitter.com/johnblakepub twitter

First published in paperback in 2011

ISBN: 978 1 84358 317 2

British Library Cataloguing-in-Publication Data:

A catalogue record for this book is available from the British Library.

Design by www.envydesign.co.uk

Printed in Great Britain by CPI Mackays, Chatham, ME5 8TD

1 3 5 7 9 10 8 6 4 2

Papers used by John Blake Publishing are natural, recyclable products
made from wood grown in sustainable forests. The manufacturing processes
conform to the environmental regulations of the country of origin.

For the truth

ACKNOWLEDGEMENTS

Many thanks to Frank Kelly and John Patrick Maher for their help in understanding the complexities of Northern Ireland, and the resources of the Pat Finucane Centre and British Irish Rights Watch.

CONTENTS

INTRODUCTION

The murder of human and civil rights lawyers is an atrocity we usually associate with countries such as Russia and China, where such rights are known to be very limited by the State. When it happens in the United Kingdom, the longest-established democracy in the world, it is shocking. However, much of the public is probably not aware of the murders of Rosemary Nelson in 1999 and Patrick Finucane in 1989. These acts are difficult to take in at first, considering that they occurred in a place covered by British law, even if the security laws in Northern Ireland were far more extreme than in other parts of Britain in this period and before. The fact that it is alleged that the British State and the security forces representing it were involved in these murders is even more shocking. This book is an examination of these events, to try to understand who really killed Rosemary Nelson.

As Richard Belfield points out in his 2005 book *The*

Secret History of Assassination, regarding alleged State involvement with terrorist or paramilitary groups in Northern Ireland during the Troubles, 'For the most part, the war was confined within the paramilitaries on both sides who were regularly culled through assassination, much of which was organised and manipulated by MI5, the Army and the Royal Ulster Constabulary (RUC) Special Branch (though they did not work together and ran their own internecine wars against each other).'

This is the background to the murder of the prominent human rights lawyer Rosemary Nelson, and another human rights lawyer, Patrick Finucane, killed ten years before her. Both of them were known as 'Republicans'; both were Catholics, but represented both Republicans and Loyalists. There are allegations made against both in this book, mainly that they were both allegedly involved or at least associated with paramilitary groups themselves. These allegations have never been proven, but it is up to the reader to make up his or her own mind.

However, the allegation that the British Government, through the Royal Ulster Constabulary (RUC) (the Northern Ireland police force run by the British), security services (chiefly MI5) and the Army were involved in their murders or allowed them to happen, or failed to prevent them when they allegedly could have done so, is very troubling. The evidence presented here is very complex and must be read with caution, allowing for political agendas and propaganda. But there are many questions to be answered, and sometimes there seems to be reluctance on the parts of the above parties to supply answers.

This book has no political agenda or bias and only aims to get as close to the truth as possible. Atrocities committed and allegedly committed by parties on both sides of the Northern Ireland sectarian divide are covered, but the main focus is on Loyalist paramilitaries, as they carried out the murder of Rosemary Nelson. Also, to address the question of alleged State collusion in her murder, there is an examination of how the security services, especially the RUC, operated on the ground at that time.

This book is about who killed Rosemary Nelson. We know with almost absolute certainty that the actual action of her murder was carried out by a Loyalist paramilitary group. The murder of Patrick Finucane is also threaded throughout this book, as it has many parallels with Nelson's murder. He, too, was killed by a Loyalist paramilitary. However, the main focus of this examination into who is responsible for those two killings is not to identify the specific individuals who physically carried out the acts (although in the interests of justice these killers need to be brought to trial). The thrust of this book is an analysis of how they could be murdered, and whether there was any alleged State involvement or collusion in their murders. This is set against the background of the Troubles, through which they both lived, although Rosemary Nelson was killed less than a year after the Good Friday Agreement in April 1998. At the time of the agreement, then British Prime Minister Tony Blair said, 'I feel the hand of history on my shoulder.'

But did Rosemary Nelson feel the heavy hand of the British State on her shoulder?

PROLOGUE

15 MARCH 1999
Lurgan, County Armagh, Northern Ireland

A residential street in a tiny town just 18 miles (29km) south-west of Belfast. The street is wide and straight with cottages lining it. In the distance, the faint sound of children playing in the nearby primary school can be heard. Otherwise, it is quiet with the deserted feeling of daytime when most are at work or school, and others doing household chores. But there is always an underlying tension in the air here, one that cannot always be seen or touched, that exists between Roman Catholics and Protestants. This street sits firmly in a Catholic nationalist community. A petite blonde woman emerges from the front door of her home. Her daughter is one of those playing in the primary school playground. It's 12.40pm.

The woman's name is Rosemary Nelson. She is 40 years old, a solicitor who has made a name for herself in Northern Ireland and America in the last few years as a human rights campaigner through her legal work. She also does a lot of work with women suffering domestic abuse and with child-custody issues. But she is famous in her world because she has been representing some high-profile figures involved in the Troubles, which still rage on in a splintered fashion despite the signing of the Good Friday Agreement the previous year. She has represented both Republican and Loyalist clients. Her face is well known on television and in newspapers here.

Rosemary Nelson climbs into her silver BMW. It is sometimes her practice to leave for work around midday, having worked from home in the morning. She always phones ahead to her office to tell her staff she's on her way. The thoughts in her head are everyday thoughts, about work and family. She is married to Paul and their children are Gavin aged 13, Christopher aged 11 and Sarah aged 8.

She starts the car and drives towards the junction opposite Tannaghmore Primary School where her daughter Sarah is wrapped up in her childhood world. Her mother Rosemary inhabits a far more complex world, one in which she has been receiving death threats against her and members of her family for some time both from Loyalist paramilitaries and allegedly from individual officers from the RUC, the latter allegedly sending veiled threats to her through her clients. It is her persistence in fighting human rights abuses, the dogged representation of some politically and religiously divisive clients and the information she is alleged to have passed to them that have made her a target. Later allegations would be made against Rosemary Nelson, that she was a 'terrorist' herself, and that she was allegedly having an affair with one of her clients.

Rosemary Nelson has lived under this dark cloud for some time. Just a few months ago, in the autumn of 1998, she travelled to Washington to testify before the US Congress about the situation in Northern Ireland. She stated there that she had received multiple warnings and that she felt threatened.

She is now at the junction, her daughter playing at her school just yards away. She applies the brakes, a routine action that will have disastrous consequences.

One of the death threats that Rosemary Nelson received is stark in its lack of ambiguity: 'We have you in our sights, you republican bastard... we will teach you a lesson. RIP'

TEN YEARS EARLIER
12 February 1989
North Belfast

A handsome, 39-year-old lawyer called Patrick Finucane sits having Sunday dinner with his family in their home. Around the dining table are his wife Geraldine and three children. Finucane is well known locally for representing paramilitary clients of both Republican/Nationalist and Loyalist persuasions, and has won several landmark human rights rulings against the British Government. His most prominent client was the legendary Republican hunger-striker Bobby Sands, who starved to death over 66 days in the Maze Prison in 1981. It's 7.25pm when his wife Geraldine hears a sound coming from the direction of the front door.

There's no other warning. Pat Finucane springs up from the table and opens the kitchen door, his wife now standing behind him. They see a man dressed in black walking towards them down the hall. He is wearing black gauntlets on his arms, with a combat jacket tied around his waist, a gun in his hand. Geraldine reaches behind her husband and hits the silent panic alarm behind the kitchen door, installed by a security company because of the nature of Pat's job. Pat closes the kitchen door, but what happens next becomes a blur. The masked man bursts in, and nobody sees a second man, although two guns will be used, a 9mm-P Browning, the other a .38 Special or .357 Magnum revolver.

The gunman opens rapid fire immediately and then sprays slower, more considered shots, firing twelve rounds into Pat Finucane, hitting him six times in the head, three times in the neck and three times in the upper body, also hitting his wife in the ankle with a ricocheting bullet. In a matter of moments, Pat Finucane is lying dead on his back on the floor, and his assassin has gone. The children look on in sheer terror, but they are mercifully physically unhurt. Geraldine hobbles to the hall and manages to call the police, who arrive five minutes later at 7.35pm.

The Loyalist organisations – the Ulster Defence Association (UDA) and the Ulster Freedom Fighters (UFF) – later take responsibility for Finucane's murder, claiming that he was a high-ranking member of the Irish Republican Army (IRA). Many suspect that the RUC was in some way linked to the killing. Fourteen years later, in 2003, the Stevens Report into Finucane's killing carried out by the British Government concluded that the Northern Ireland police did collude in his murder. However, the RUC had been disbanded in 2001 to be replaced by the Police Service of Northern Ireland (PSNI).

Geraldine Finucane is rushed to hospital and treated, and recovers physically but she and the three children will have to live with the indelible image of having witnessed the husband and father they loved being gunned down in front of them.

1

A LAWYER IN
THE LAIR

In the same year that Pat Finucane was executed in North Belfast, 30-year-old Rosemary Nelson set up the first solicitor's office run by a woman in Lurgan, the small town where she was born to the south-west of Belfast. Independent of spirit and dedicated to her law practice that soon took on staff, Rosemary built up a fine reputation in her local community. It was only later that her fame would spread far wider.

Rosemary's practice also helped run an advice and health centre on a Lurgan housing estate. As her sister Caitlin told the *Irish News* in March 2003, 'There were all types of people going to her. There were a lot of separations, domestic disputes. Women who were in difficult situations. And she would have gone out of her way for people. She would not just treat them as clients.' Rosemary would often do extra work for clients free of charge, becoming involved in their problems, and this commitment to those in need made her very popular and trusted.

Rosemary Nelson had a remarkable skill for empathy. She could relate to other people and their feelings, a key skill for a solicitor dealing with families. Like all of us, Rosemary's life experiences made her the person she became.

Rosemary Magee was born on Lurgan's Shore Road on 4 September 1958. Her family was well established in the area and, like in any very small town, the inhabitants were familiar with each other and knew each other's business. It is a flat landscape on the south-east shore of Lough Neagh, and the name Lurgan comes from the Irish 'an Lorgain' meaning 'the long ridge' where the oldest part of the town still sits today. At the time of the 1961 census, just three years after Rosemary's birth, Lurgan, Armagh, had a population of 17,872, and 40 years later in 2001 this had only grown to 23,534, small by any standards. The town's origins were as a Plantation of Ulster settlement in the early seventeenth century and, in 1610, the lands of Lurgan were gifted to Lord William Brownlow, an Englishman. By 1619, the Brownlow family had built a castle, and records held with the Craigavon Historical Society show that at that time the streets were already paved and there were 42 houses, as well as a watermill and windmill.

In 1639, William Brownlow became MP for Armagh in the Irish Parliament. Two years later, during the Irish Rebellion, Brownlow's castle was destroyed and he and his family were imprisoned for a year, their land being given to two Irish families – the O'Hanlons and the McCanns. But the Brownlows did go back to Lurgan after their liberation by Lord Conway and continued to be a presence in the town, Brownlow himself dying in 1660.

From that period onwards, Lurgan became a textile town, producing linen, and this remained the main local employer until the late twentieth century when clothing production in the developing world meant that it was no longer profitable to produce it in towns such as Lurgan.

Lurgan would also play a significant role in the Troubles in Northern Ireland from the 1960s on. Along with the nearby towns of Craigavon and Portadown, it became part of what was known as the 'murder triangle' because of the amount of fatalities which took place there. Lurgan is unusual in Northern Ireland (although not unique) for having a long history of a significant support base for both Republicans and Loyalists and therefore the potential for respective dissident activities, which continues to this day. As recently as 14 August 2010, a bomb planted by dissident Republicans exploded in a public bin in Lurgan and injured three children.

There is an expression in Northern Ireland: 'to have a face as long as a Lurgan spade', meaning to look miserable. This is not literal and has its disputed origins in far more obscure roots. Those wide Lurgan streets where Rosemary Magee was born in 1958 on Shore Road had far from a 'miserable' new arrival. Rosemary would grow into a woman of spirit, great humour and determination.

But Rosemary developed into a warm and extrovert child against the odds, and perhaps it was partly those odds that made her different from other children. She was born with a large strawberry birthmark down the left side of her face. This singled her out from other children but did not make her introverted, due to the love and support of her mother and father, four sisters and two brothers, of whom Rosemary was the middle child.

She attended Tannaghmore Primary School, where her own children would later go, and did well there with her schoolwork, as well as making a close circle of friends. These were the strong foundations of Rosemary's later highly respected place in the Lurgan community.

From the age of ten, she began a number of skin-graft operations to have the birthmark removed from her face. The medical procedures of the times meant that this involved prolonged and painful surgery after which she would be hospitalised and would need several recuperation periods of up to 15 weeks. This meant that she missed a great deal of school, but, despite this, at St Michael's Grammar School where she went after Tannaghmore, she regularly got top grades. Rosemary was a bright girl with a lively, inquisitive mind, all attributes that would make her a highly effective lawyer.

It is even more impressive that she continued to succeed academically and remained a cheerful, outgoing personality because the surgeries did remove the birthmark, but unfortunately paralysed the left side of her face. For the rest of her life, her face would noticeably droop down on that side, her left eye pulled down out of alignment with the right. This would have destroyed the confidence of many young women at a very self-conscious time in their lives, but not Rosemary. She was swiftly becoming one of life's survivors, but whose great tenacity would also lead her into treacherous waters in the future.

Rosemary appeared unaffected by her disfigurement, and this was no doubt largely due to the loving support of her family and friends. However, on a deeply personal or even subconscious level, it must have made her something of an outsider. Any developing person would be similarly affected. We are conditioned to fit into our society and anything that makes us different singles us out, especially in early years. It is to Rosemary's great credit that she turned a difficult start into a positive future, and one of considerable achievement.

There was a positive side-effect, however, and one that would make her the woman and lawyer she became: Rosemary developed a great empathy and understanding of others, particularly those who were persecuted and in distress. But again, ultimately, this would also lead her to take on more, perhaps, than any individual might reasonably have done in her situation.

Rosemary's childhood was a happy one, though, apart from dealing with her disfigurement psychologically and emotionally. She was a lively and inquisitive girl growing up at the height of the Troubles in a place where they could not be ignored. Her family told the *Irish News* in 2003 that she was not 'political', rather 'politically aware'. This was not unusual in that time and place, as every child had to understand the basics of the Troubles, although not the great complexities. To survive took knowledge, and Rosemary was no different in arming herself with it. But Rosemary was also interested in current affairs on the international stage, not just in Northern Ireland.

Rosemary did well at secondary school and was able to speak fluent Irish, and would speak it with her brother Eunan, who would later go on to teach the Irish language. They were the only members of the family who could speak it, and they would use it as a 'secret' language between them and then get told off for doing it.

Her teenage summers were spent with the family on idyllic holidays in beautiful Co Donegal, part of a well-balanced childhood.

With a probing mind and a thirst for knowledge, it was little wonder that Rosemary went on to Queen's University, Belfast. She studied Law there, and it was soon obvious that she had found a subject and a vocation brilliantly suited to her personality and intellect. She graduated from there with a good degree in 1981, and went on to work for two law firms, along the way meeting her future husband Paul Nelson, with whom she would have three children: Gavin, Christopher and Sarah.

In 1989, Rosemary Nelson opened her own legal practice at 8 William Street, Lurgan, and became a pioneer as the first woman to do so in the town. She was very hard working and took her job very seriously, but also greatly valued her family and always tried to balance her work and family life. If she had been born in a town in another part of the country, Rosemary Nelson would probably have spent her career as a well-respected solicitor dealing in everyday domestic issues. Instead, she became an internationally renowned human rights lawyer, the cost of which was representing some very controversial clients and cases in a troubled time and place.

Rosemary Nelson's transition from representing ordinary clients with everyday problems and disputes to defending high-profile, politically dissident clients was a slow and organic one. To understand this, it needs to be reiterated that Lurgan was in the middle of the Troubles and had been for decades. With such a divided Roman Catholic and Protestant community (although some locals have overcome this divide for many years), there were bound to be approaches to Rosemary to take on more controversial cases. The fact that she agreed to act as a lawyer in these cases is controversial in itself, however.

There would later be claims that Rosemary was more than just a lawyer. Although she did, in fact, represent both Republican and Loyalist clients, it was the former that made the headlines. Along with an allegation that she had had an affair with her most high-profile Republican client and allegedly had even passed information about pending cases to the IRA itself, there is a grey area which cannot be ignored and will be explored in this book.

Rosemary Nelson's personality is also key to her accepting these clients, of course. Her family has attested that she found it impossible to turn away anyone in need, irrespective of their alleged activities and ties. She had a strong sense of justice and a good lawyer pursues that above all else, especially when there are suspected human rights abuses, just as a good doctor's mission is to treat and cure the sick. Whether Rosemary did more than this (as the authorities and Loyalists claim) is another 'grey area' in these hugely complex circumstances.

Perspective must be kept, however – Rosemary's practice continued to represent ordinary people with their problems throughout the 1990s. But it is the more divisive clients that changed her life and that of her family. As her brother Eunan told the *Irish News* in 2003 about his sister, 'She certainly wasn't naïve, but maybe underestimated the way things would develop. I think she would then want to follow it to its logical end.' Four key cases illustrate this growing controversy surrounding her client base.

Colin Duffy, a Lurgan man, has always admitted to

being a mainstream Republican but strongly denied being an IRA member. However, according to the *Sunday World* newspaper, MI5 'placed him at the top of a dissident Republican cell in the Craigavon and Lurgan areas of Co Armagh'. Back in January 1990, when he was in his early twenties, Duffy and his friends Sam Marshall and Tony McCaughey were at McCaughey's house when it was raided by the RUC. Arrested and charged with having ten bullets in their possession, Duffy and Marshall were granted bail the following month, but McCaughey wasn't released on bail until March. The conditions of their bail were that they had to sign on at the local Lurgan RUC barracks twice a week. They went to their first signing together on 7 March but, as they left the barracks, a red Maestro car followed them, this car also being seen by independent witnesses. Tony McCaughey later described the driver as being smartly dressed in a dark suit and white shirt. Then the Maestro passed them, swiftly followed by a red Rover, and this car would pass them again on their way towards Lurgan town centre. The Rover was finally seen parked.

Duffy, Marshall and McCaughey were now very concerned and chose to follow a different route, but then two masked men jumped out of the Rover and opened fire on them. Sam Marshall was hit and therefore unable to run. The gunmen finished Marshall off on the ground with two shots to the head. Duffy and McCaughey were very lucky to escape unscathed.

It has never been proven that there was a tip-off, although the time of their bail signings were known only to them, their solicitor and the RUC. The Rover car was discovered burned out close to the M1 motorway.

Four years later, in 1994, RUC Inspector Alan Clegg divulged in an extradition hearing in the United States that the red Maestro had been an intelligence services car. He also added that on the fateful night it was part of an RUC surveillance operation, one of three cars, one of which had belonged to the RUC.

Sam Marshall's family is still campaigning for a full open inquest into his death, and Rosemary Nelson supported their cause. Republican supporters of Colin Duffy cite his knowledge of what happened that night as a motivation for individual officers from the RUC, and subsequently the PSNI, allegedly hounding Duffy in order to get him off the streets and prevent him from giving evidence in any such inquest. But, of course, as with any political viewpoint, this has to be approached in a balanced way, allowing for partisan agendas.

Three years after Sam Marshall's murder, Colin Duffy was again in the spotlight. On 24 June 1993, an Ulster Defence Regiment (UDR) soldier, 57-year-old John Lyness, was shot dead outside his home in Lime Grove, Lurgan, by the IRA. Lyness had retired from the UDR the previous year after 20 years of service. Lyness had just parked his car and, seeing his two killers approach, was able to pull out his 'personal protection weapon', but the gunmen shot first. Colin Duffy was soon charged with the murder. It was at this time that Rosemary Nelson began representing Colin Duffy.

One of the key witnesses against Duffy was a Unionist/Loyalist called Lindsay Robb. Robb gave evidence at the trial from behind a screen, saying that he saw Duffy in the vicinity of Lime Grove at the time of the shooting. Duffy would go on to serve three years in prison before Rosemary got him out in 1996, after Lindsay Robb was unmasked as an Ulster Voluntary Force (UVF) member and arrested for gun-running on their behalf in Scotland, Rosemary winning her argument that Robb's evidence was no longer credible.

In 2000, Robb would make dramatic allegations about RUC involvement in Duffy's conviction. Robb said that RUC Special Branch had approached the UVF, asking them to give them a 'clean' witness to frame Duffy. Robb said that Special Branch had insinuated that they would 'go easy' on the UVF and their operations in Mid-Ulster if this service was provided. Robb explained that a senior member of the UVF had come to him and asked him to testify against Duffy, which he did.

Colin Duffy said, 'If the RUC were prepared to collude with Loyalists to take me out in 1993, then it is reasonable to assume that members of the British Crown forces were involved in the UVF's attempt to take me out in 1990. This was not the first or last time RUC Special Branch or some other section of the British Crown forces were in contact with Loyalist paramilitaries.'

However, Lindsay Robb told the *Sunday Herald* in 2000, 'My evidence against Duffy was part of a deal struck with loyalist terrorists – namely the UVF – and the RUC. I want to make it clear that my evidence was not perjured. I stand by the fact that I saw Duffy in the vicinity of the murder, but I would not have come forward without the request of the UVF following approaches made by the RUC.' Therefore, Robb was maintaining his account of the murder of John Lyness, although it must be borne in mind that his evidence had been found not to be credible subsequent to the original trial. But his allegations about RUC collusion with the UVF are very concerning. Rosemary Nelson echoed this allegation of RUC collusion in 1997, years before the outpourings of the Loyalist Lindsay Robb. She brought up the alleged collusion in the 1990 murder of Sam Marshall, too, in support of his family's campaign.

Fast-forward a year. In July 1997, Duffy was accused of killing two RUC constables – Roland John Graham and David Andrew Johnston – the previous month in Lurgan. He was arrested and charged, and spent several months in prison. Witnesses came forward to place Duffy elsewhere at the time of the murders, but this was not enough to prove his innocence to the court. In the end, Rosemary managed to get the case dropped by showing that a mentally unstable woman had been 'pressurised' by the RUC into giving evidence against Duffy. The Director of Public Prosecutions (DPP) said that there was less than 'a reasonable chance' of getting a conviction. Rosemary received death threats after this high-profile legal victory and allegations were made that she had had an affair with Duffy and that she had passed sensitive legal information to the IRA through him and others. Duffy has always strenuously denied being a member of the IRA (though he does admit to being a Republican). He has also consistently denied having an affair with Rosemary Nelson.

But Duffy continued to make headlines after he stopped being Rosemary Nelson's client. In 2001, the police, probing the 1989 murder of 40-year-old Roy Metcalfe, a Protestant army-surplus shop owner, raided Duffy's home. Metcalfe had been shot 18 times. A pair of boots had been found at the scene of Metcalfe's murder, and Duffy's shoes were seized for forensic analysis.

On 7 March 2009, an event occurred in Antrim town that has become known as the 'Massereene Barracks Shooting'. At about 9.40pm, four off-duty (and therefore unarmed) British soldiers wearing desert fatigues (they were due to go to Afghanistan the next day) came to the gates of their barracks to collect pizzas they had ordered. Just as the delivery was being handed over by two Polish pizza-delivery men, gunfire erupted from a nearby green Vauxhall Cavalier car. Two men in the car were shooting at the soldiers with Heckler & Koch G3A3 battle rifles. The shots rang out for over 30 seconds, more than 60 shots being fired, after wounding the soldiers with the initial volleys, and opening fire again to finish them off. Sapper Patrick Azimkar from London and Sapper Mark Quinsey from Birmingham were killed, while the other two soldiers and both delivery men were injured.

Within hours, the Vauxhall Cavalier was found abandoned eight miles away in Randalstown. Then the *Sunday Tribune* newspaper in Dublin received a message using a Real IRA codeword claiming responsibility for the shootings, saying that the Polish delivery men were legitimate targets as they were 'collaborating with the British by servicing them'. The incident was especially high profile because Quinsey and Azimkar were the first British soldiers to be killed in Northern Ireland for 12 years, since February 1997 when Lance Bombardier Stephen Restorick was killed by the 'South Armagh Sniper', a generic term referring to the specialist sniping teams that were mobilised in the area. Rosemary Nelson also represented one man alleged to be actively involved.

A week after the Massereene Barracks Shooting, on 14 March 2009, 41-year-old Colin Duffy was arrested along with two others. By this time, Duffy had left the fold of mainstream Republicanism by criticising the IRA's political wing Sinn Fein for supporting the PSNI, formed to replace the RUC. On 25 March, following a judicial review, all three men were released by the Belfast High Court. However, Duffy alone was immediately rearrested and the next day charged with the murders of Sappers Azimkar and Quinsey and the attempted murder of five others. When indicted, it was alleged that Duffy's full DNA profile was identified on a latex glove found in the glove compartment of the Vauxhall Cavalier used by the shooters, a billion-to-one chance of it not being left there by him, it is claimed. In July 2009, a 44-year-old called Brian Shivers was also charged in connection with the shootings after being arrested in Mid-Ulster.

Colin Duffy is currently awaiting trial in the high security Maghaberry Prison in Lisburn, Northern Ireland, and continues to profess his innocence, while protesting about alleged human rights abuses inside the prison.

It must be remembered, however, that the Republican/Nationalist movement was guilty of many murders in this period, and the use of snipers was very prevalent, following the motto of 'one shot, one kill'. Around 180 British soldiers, members of the RUC and prison staff were killed by IRA and associated dissident Republican group snipers between 1971 and 1991. That is not to mention civilian casualties. Perhaps the most shocking was the butchering of 29 people (including 9 children and a woman pregnant with twins) in bomb blasts in the high street of Omagh on 15 August 1998, by the Real IRA, an offshoot of the Provisional IRA, who were then under a ceasefire. In considering the Troubles up to the signing of the Good Friday Agreement in 1998 and subsequent paramilitary activity, the conscience of both Loyalist and Republican sides is far from clear. Even if they considered themselves 'at war', civilian women and children surely can never be regarded as legitimate targets.

Another client of Rosemary Nelson who would make headlines was Michael Caraher, suspected of being part of the South Armagh Sniper. Operational from 1990 to 1997, the name sounds like the work of an individual, but actually involved two sniper teams working under the aegis of the Provisional IRA. The targets of the snipers were the British security forces, namely the British Army (comprising of several army sections and an SAS unit) and the RUC. In this seven-year period, the South Armagh Sniper killed seven soldiers, two RUC constables and wounded one other RUC constable. The IRA even erected a road sign near Crossmaglen reading 'Sniper at Work'.

The two sniper teams making up the South Armagh Sniper used long-range rifles, the .50 BMG calibre Barrett M82 and M90 particularly. It has been established that, while during the 1980s the main source of IRA arms came from Libya, by 1990 the main source was the United States, the above rifles being manufactured there. In his 1999 book *Bandit Country: The IRA & South Armagh*, the journalist and author Toby Harnden quoted an anonymous IRA volunteer on the power of the rifles: 'What's special about the Barrett is the huge kinetic energy. The bullet can just walk through a flak jacket. South Armagh was the prime place to use such weapons because of the availability of Brits. They came to dread it and that was part of its effectiveness.'

As well as taking out targets, the South Armagh Sniper

certainly brought fear, although the British Army reported that the skills of the IRA marksmen often did not equal those of a well-trained sniper. However, the activities of the Sniper, as well as the fatalities and wounding inflicted, caused the security forces to redirect their resources and disrupted its routine operations, including the use of helicopters which were vulnerable to sniper attacks.

The two teams of the South Armagh Sniper consisted of one covering the eastern side of South Armagh, the other the west. Each team consisted of at least four snipers, but there were many other logistical and scouting volunteers. The snipers normally fired from a range of less than 300m, although the Barrett rifles are capable of a range of 1km. It is estimated that 16 missions were carried out from the back of a vehicle, with the sniper(s) behind an armoured plate in case of return of fire. From 1990 up to mid-1992, the first eight missions carried out by the Sniper missed their targets, but the hit rate soon improved, the first victim, Private Paul Turner, being killed at Crossmaglen on 28 August 1992. The year 1993 was the most prolific for the Sniper, seeing seven fatalities. The ninth and last fatality attributed to the South Armagh Sniper, the murder of Lance Bombardier Stephen Restorick at Bessbrook on 12 February 1997, was described by Sinn Fein leader Gerry Adams as 'tragic', and Adams even wrote a letter of condolence to Restorick's mother.

The sniper team covering the eastern side of Southern Armagh was never to be caught, but the one covering the west was apprehended by the SAS on 10 April 1997. There was a brief struggle without shots being fired (the

SAS were under orders to avoid casualties), and Bernard McGinn, James McCardle, Michael Caraher and Martin Minnes were arrested on a farm close to Freeduff. A Barrett M90 rifle was found with them, later linked to shootings that had taken place in 1997, including the serious wounding of an RUC constable who almost lost his leg as a result. One of the snipers, Michael Caraher, was suspected of taking part in several shootings, but was indicted on the charge of the wounding of the RUC constable. His lawyer was Rosemary Nelson.

The story that led to Michael Caraher's involvement was common in the Troubles on both sides of the political/religious divide. There was reinforced hatred of the British among Republicans and of each other on both sides, the feeling of bad blood running in families, sometimes justifiably in the internecine complexities of a war. Michael Caraher's brother Fergal was a member of Sinn Fein who had been killed by Royal Marines at a checkpoint near Cullyhanna on 30 December 1990. Michael had also been present and was wounded, later losing a lung as a result. Witnesses stated that the shootings had not been provoked, but Lord Chief Justice Hutton, having considered all the evidence, acquitted the Royal Marines.

Rosemary Nelson did not manage to get an acquittal for Caraher, however. The evidence against him was too strong. McCardle, Minnes and McGinn were convicted of six killings, two of them not in South Armagh, but in Canary Wharf, London, where McCardle planted a bomb in 1996.

All four of the South Armagh Sniper team went to prison but were released under the terms of the Good Friday Agreement in 2001, having served just 18 months.

Another high-profile case taken on by Rosemary Nelson in the mid- to late 1990s was her representation of the Garvaghy Road Residents Coalition (GRRC) in the Drumcree Conflict. This centred on the violent dispute over a march through that part of the town of Portadown, not far from Lurgan. The Orange Order (linked to the Loyalist Unionists) had marched through Drumcree past the church since 1807. However, the area around Drumcree has been a highly populated Catholic/Nationalist area for some time (although Portadown as a whole is mainly Protestant), and there had been violence surrounding the march since 1873, and this became worse after the Troubles started in 1969. Local Catholics felt that the parade through their town by Protestants was 'triumphalist' and 'supremacist', exacerbated by local Protestants displaying their Unionist flags during the march. The Orange Order denied this and cited its historical right to take their parade along the traditional route, which takes place on the Sunday before 12 July every year.

Until the 1990s, the most controversial leg of the route was the outward one along Obins Street, but the parade was diverted away from this area in 1986. Subsequently, the return route along Garvaghy Road became the focus of outrage. In 1995, the dispute really kicked off, sparking riots and protests across Northern Ireland which was reported internationally and would be repeated every year until 1998. At least five civilians died during this rioting, and this led to an enormous operation by the security forces around the time of the march every year.

Rosemary Nelson became involved with the GRRC soon after the dispute intensified. In 1997, then Northern

Ireland Secretary Mo Mowlam tried to broker peace between the Orange Order and the GRRC to avoid further unrest. That year, the decision to let the march go through the Garvaghy Road had been made a month before, but Rosemary Nelson had continued to petition Mo Mowlam to prevent that leg of the march going through up until midnight of the night before the event. There was no response from Dr Mowlam and she could not be located.

In 2009, the former Chief Constable of the RUC, Sir Ronnie Flanagan, claimed that the GRRC had planned to 'kidnap' Mo Mowlam on a planned visit to the area in that year. Flanagan said, 'There was intelligence to suggest that if she went to the road there was risk that she would be held hostage by the residents, although there was no intelligence to suggest her life was in danger.' A spokesman for the GRRC responded by saying that the claim was 'sheer fantasy' and that 'Mo Mowlam had never any intentions of visiting the Garvaghy Road'.

In 1998, the march was prohibited from going through the Garvaghy Road and the majority of the Nationalist area.

It was during the height of the Drumcree Conflict and the furore over the march of the Orange Order down Garvaghy Road that a terrible incident occurred that would give Rosemary Nelson another controversial case to represent. It happened in the town of Portadown where the march dispute was in full flow, against the background of these heightened sectarian tensions.

It was at around 1.30am in the early morning of 27 April 1997 that four young people, two men and two women, were walking down Market Street, a main street in Portadown on their way back from a Catholic dance.

They were a father of three, 25-year-old Robert Hamill, his friend Gregory Girvan and two of his cousins, Joanne and Siobhan Girvan, the former also being Gregory's wife. Approaching the main crossroads of the town, the four saw a group of about 30 people (both men and women) congregated around the crossroads. It was a location that had seen disturbances in the past, and the four young Catholics did think twice about carrying on, particularly because of the ongoing violence that had engulfed the area over the previous two years because of the Drumcree Conflict. But something they saw made them feel safer, and so they carried on.

It was an RUC Land Rover parked near the crossroads, not far from the group of Loyalists grouped nearby. As Amnesty International pointed out in a report in October 1999, another Catholic man had left the dance a little earlier and, on feeling intimidated by the presence of the Loyalists, had asked the RUC officers to 'keep an eye out' for other Catholics coming out of the hall. But the confidence that Hamill, Gregory, Joanne and Siobhan Girvan placed in the RUC that night was proved to be misplaced.

As the four got to the crossroads at Market Street and Thomas Street, the 30-strong group pounced on them. Robert Hamill and Gregory Girvan were beaten to the ground and brutally kicked. Hamill got the worst of it and fell unconscious almost immediately. But his attackers continued to kick him on the ground, shouting, 'Die, you Fenian bastard.' ('Fenian' is a traditional word for a Republican.)

Joanne and Siobhan Girvan would later swear that they called out to the RUC officers inside the Land Rover begging for help. The four RUC officers were approximately 20ft away from the attack, but they did not try to stop the violence. They did reportedly call an ambulance, but this took several more minutes to arrive. Siobhan Girvan had by now thrown herself on to Robert Hamill to shield him, and one of the RUC officers did tell her to turn Robert on to his side into the recovery position. In all, the attack lasted about ten minutes.

Robert Hamill was rushed to hospital and found to have a severe head injury. He never regained consciousness, and died on 8 May 1997, 12 days later. Gregory Girvan suffered facial cuts and severe bruising in the attack.

The first statements given out by the RUC stated that there had been a 'battle' between Loyalist and Republican groups, which certainly was not the case (although later they said that it was a large group of Loyalists against four Catholics). There had been around 30 male and female Loyalists and only four Republicans, two of them women. It had been an ambush, pure and simple. It was added that it would not have been safe for the RUC to intervene. But had they called for reinforcements? To top that, no evidence was gathered at the crime scene despite the presence of the four police officers throughout the incident and in the aftermath after the ambulance had arrived. Even more strangely, nobody was arrested that early morning or immediately afterwards.

Detective Inspector Irwen of the local Portadown RUC unit led the investigation into the murder of Robert Hamill, the same unit to which the four RUC officers in the Land Rover were attached; inevitably, there were concerns about the independence of such an investigation.

Six people were eventually arrested for Hamill's murder and they were held in custody in the Maze, where they requested they be held in the Loyalist Volunteer Force (LVF) wing of the prison. The Maze had segregated wings and subsection wings for the corresponding sectarian groups and organisations, and the six were undoubtedly very concerned about Republican reprisals inside the prison, which were not uncommon. Their request was granted but, by November 1997, just seven months after the murder, only one of the six suspects was still in prison – Paul Rodney Marc Hobson – who was charged with the murder of Robert Hamill. The other five were released as there was said to be insufficient evidence to get murder convictions, and the magistrate who released them offered his sympathy for the ordeal of their time in custody.

In March 1999, Paul Hobson was acquitted of Hamill's murder due to lack of evidence, but Hobson was sentenced to four years in prison for affray. The trial judge said that 'it is probable that [Hobson] intended and did strike' Hamill. Nobody ever stood trial for the attack on Gregory Girvan.

Regarding the four RUC officers in the Land Rover, the judge stated that he was 'unable to resolve the question whether police officers remained in the Land Rover during the attack.' He did add that due to the evidence amassed from civilian witness statements 'this would not be entirely surprising and would necessarily reflect on the officers' commitment to duty' since there was apparently no warning that violence would flare up. However, the judge did reprimand the four RUC officers for not 'anticipating' the attack, given three reasons: (i) their disregard of the message given by the man who had approached them after leaving the dance hall just a short time before the attack, asking them to watch out for any Catholics coming out; (ii) for parking their Land Rover in a place where they did not have a clear overview of the junction, and staying there even after receiving the man's warning; (iii) their failure to act on information given to them at the scene about a man, against whom a *prima facie* case could have been built.

The four RUC officers were not suspended from duty after the attack. Robert Hamill's family made an official complaint against the RUC for the failure of their officers to act or react to the attack.

At this stage, Rosemary Nelson became the Hamill family's lawyer. An investigation into the conduct of the four RUC officers was instigated and supervised by the ICPC. However, this is a regulatory body and has no investigators of its own, so the investigation was carried out by the RUC itself and the findings passed to the ICPC. The ICPC inquiry into Robert Hamill's murder was conducted again on the ground by members of the Portadown RUC unit, the very unit to which the four RUC officers under scrutiny belonged, just as the initial criminal investigation had been.

These officers were not suspended while the investigation was under way (the reason given was that they had not broken any operational rules. This was even after the gathering of a petition containing 20,000 signatures calling for their suspension by the Hamill family with the help of Rosemary Nelson and presented to the then Secretary of State for Northern Ireland, Dr Mo Mowlam. In its 1997 Annual Report, the ICPC stated that there were 'several opportunities' for witnesses to be interviewed regarding the Hamill murder, but that only one person had attended. As Amnesty International pointed out, could this be because the RUC itself was undertaking the investigation on the ground?

That was not the end of it. Rosemary Nelson began mounting private proceedings against the six murder suspects and alleged RUC collusion, and this will be examined later.

On 19 January 1998, the ICPC made a statement saying that it was satisfied with the handling of the criminal investigation into Hamill's murder, and its report was then passed to the DPP. On 29 September, the DPP made the decision not to bring any charges against the RUC officers 'for their alleged failure to protect Robert Hamill and his companions'. This was apparently due to the fact that it was unlikely that any convictions would follow. The only legal avenue left open to the Hamill family was civil proceedings against the RUC. As mentioned earlier, the RUC was disbanded in 2001, to be replaced by the PSNI.

In October 1999, Amnesty International published a report into the murder of Robert Hamill called 'The Sectarian Killing of Robert Hamill'. It reads: 'Amnesty International is concerned about the alleged failure of RUC officers to intervene and protect Robert Hamill and his companions... about the failure of the RUC officers to provide first aid to Robert Hamill... about the failure of the RUC to impartially and promptly investigate the attack, including the failure to preserve the scene of crime, to secure forensic evidence and to make arrests; and about misleading press statements issued by the RUC after the incident.'

Amnesty International then called for a full and impartial public inquiry into Robert Hamill's murder. At the time of writing in 2010, a public inquiry is still under way on the recommendation of the Cory Collusion Inquiry.

So, by the late 1990s, Rosemary Nelson was embroiled in some very controversial cases and her public profile was rising significantly. As we shall see, she would even testify before the US Congress in Washington about the Troubles. But to fully understand subsequent events and Rosemary Nelson's position at the centre of them, it is helpful to go back and look at a brief overview of the roots of the Troubles, the complexities of which are truly labyrinthine.

2

THE LONG TENTACLES OF THE TROUBLES

The road that led to the Good Friday Agreement in 1998 and the British Prime Minister Tony Blair's statement, 'I feel the hand of history on my shoulder…' had been a very long and treacherous one. The immense complexities of what some considered a war and others plain terrorism are too vast to explain in detail here. However, an overview of the roots of the problem and its organic relevance to Rosemary Nelson and her times is useful to try to understand the motivations for extreme actions. The most shocking and ruthless period was of course 'the Troubles', usually considered to cover the period 1969–98. During this time, there was a total of 3,524 people killed, more than half of them civilians, and it is throughout this period that Rosemary Nelson grew up and later practised law. But the seeds of the conflict go back to much earlier times.

THE SEEDS OF DIVISION

From 1608, English and Scottish people, known as 'planters', were given lands that had been seized from the native Irish government in Ulster (this was when Englishman Lord Brownlow was gifted the land around Lurgan). The vast majority of the planters were Protestant and, along with native largely Catholic resentment at this unfair redistribution of land, religion began to be divisive in what would later become known as Northern Ireland. This animosity culminated in the Irish Confederate Wars of 1641–53, the time when Lord Brownlow of Lurgan's estate was seized and his castle razed to the ground. Decades later, in 1689–91, there was the Williamite War, and the Protestants (mainly planters supported by the English and Scottish) won both wars, the latter one including the famous Battle of the Boyne in 1690.

But the Protestant military dominance did not only lead to territorial power, of course; their lands gave them massive political power, too, and the Protestants made sure that they could maintain the upper hand. They did this by passing penal laws that were largely religious in focus, but also had far-reaching legal implications, heavily restricting the jobs that Catholics could do and lands they could rent or buy. The Anglican Church of Ireland became the native church, and Catholics had no rights if they did not conform to the new status quo. This remained the case for almost a century, until the laws inhibiting the Catholics began to loosen, and territorial competition began to fester again, with Protestants known as the 'Peep O'Day Boys' making attacks on the Catholic community.

In reply, Catholics in the southern part of Ulster

formed 'The Defenders' who attacked Protestant holdings. So, by the 1790s, there were already two armed and organised sides battling for dominance, and some of those in the Protestant camp who had until then had some sympathy for the Catholics stopped showing it. The Catholic/Nationalist side also included Presbyterians and some liberal Anglicans, but the Irish Rebellion of 1798 was a failure.

The sectarian fighting between both sides was growing, and this increased animosity between the two sides was put on statute in 1801 when the Irish Parliament was dissolved and Ireland became part of the United Kingdom, or 'the Union'. The thread of this can be seen today with the Unionist parties of Northern Ireland. Added to this, the Orange Order (following William of Orange and his Protestant line) had been formed in 1795, and this also remains to this day, as shown in the Drumcree Conflict in Portadown of the mid-1990s, in which Rosemary Nelson was involved.

In 1829, campaigning by a man called Daniel O'Connell and his followers led to Catholic Emancipation, and this effectively removed most legal restrictions against Catholics, but the Irish Parliament was not resurrected, and the 'Home Rule' movement was born among Catholics and dissenters. It is important to remember that at this time Ireland was about 75 per cent Catholic, and so three-quarters of the people were still under the governance of a quarter, although, of course, they were supported by the English. Naturally, the Protestant Unionists needed the Union to remain intact, otherwise they would be greatly outnumbered. The divided lines were now set for the Troubles almost a century-and-a-half later.

The Home Rule movement came to greatest prominence in the early twentieth century and the push for limited self-government by the Irish gained momentum, although the Protestant Unionists strongly defended against it. In 1912, the Ulster Volunteers (an early forerunner of the later Ulster Volunteer Force (UVF)) was formed to this end and the Catholic Nationalists responded by forming the Irish Volunteers. Bills went through the British Parliament, in effect granting Home Rule, but were suspended by the First World War of 1914–18. But in 1916, there was the Easter Rising in Dublin by the largely Catholic Nationalists in the form of the Irish Volunteers (formed in 1913), leading to 15 of the Rising's architects, the Irish Republican Brotherhood, being executed.

The Nationalist political party Sinn Fein (later to be synonymous with Gerry Adams and Martin McGuinness) was formed, and it won a majority of Irish seats, and an Irish Parliament was created in Dublin. However, the six counties of Ulster (later Northern Ireland) unsurprisingly rejected Sinn Fein's advances and remained Unionist, although it must be remembered that there were large Catholic Nationalist communities within the Ulster counties. The Government of Ireland Act of 1920 effectively officially divided Ireland into the two regions (later countries) we know today: Northern Ireland and the Republic of Ireland. But, of course, the Nationalists saw this as an illegal act, against the will of a significant minority (roughly a third of the citizens of Ulster were Nationalist). In their eyes, without parliamentary pressure from Britain, it was doubtful if the entire six Ulster counties could have stayed Unionist.

This division did not come without a cost; between 1920 and 1922, 557 people were killed in sectarian violence, the majority Catholics as Richard English's book *A History of the IRA* tells us. This wave culminated in the assassination of the Catholic leader Michael Collins. These violent divisions were the true foundations of the later Troubles, the period that concerns us.

THE TROUBLES

Rosemary Nelson was born in September 1958, so she was ten years old when the Battle of the Bogside, a Nationalist uprising, occurred in Derry on 12 August 1969, and British troops were deployed into Northern Ireland two days later. It was actually a riot between Catholics living on Derry's 'Bogside', the Protestant 'Apprentice Boys' of Derry and the police. The rioting spread to Belfast and other areas and led to many deaths and the burning down of many homes. So, when Rosemary Nelson was beginning to travel to Scotland to have operations to remove the strawberry birthmark from her face, the Troubles were starting in her native Northern Ireland. The Battle of the Bogside was also the beginning of the debate as to whether or not the RUC had colluded at least to the extent of not intervening in the actions of Loyalists, as we have recorded with the account of the murders of Sam Marshall and Robert Hamill almost 30 years later. The question of alleged collusion is a major focus of this book and will feature more and more prominently.

In an interview with the authors, the Irish academic and novelist Dr John Patrick Maher explained just how explosive the years of the Troubles were. His forthcoming book, *Slouching towards Jerusalem:*

Reactive Nationalism in the Irish, Israeli and Palestinian Novel 1985–2005, looks at the influence of Nationalist politics on the literary mindset, including the late Troubles, and he lived in both the Republic and Northern Ireland during them. As well as murders and bombing atrocities, there was also widespread torturing employed, including 'scalpings', more reminiscent of the nineteenth-century American Wild West than a late-twentieth-century, apparently civilised, country.

While the armed struggles of both the Republic and Loyalist paramilitaries were founded on religious/political terms as a crusade, there were increasing allegations of gangsterism, racketeering and drug-dealing on both sides. These wholly criminal activities helped to cloud a murky and complex picture still further.

The Battle of the Bogside in August 1969 and the signing of the Good Friday Agreement in April 1998 were arguably the bookends of the beginning and end of the Troubles. With a slight overlap, between 1969 and 2001, 3,526 people would lose their lives, 1,857 of them civilians. The *Sutton Index of Deaths* shows us that 2,057 people were killed by Republican paramilitary groups, 1,019 by Loyalist paramilitaries, 363 by the British security forces, 5 by the Irish security forces, and 82 people killed by persons unknown. To understand the true terror of the Troubles, it is useful for us here to focus on the protagonists. This should, in turn, help us to understand Rosemary Nelson's story.

THE IRA AND OTHER REPUBLICAN PARAMILITARIES

The original Irish Republican Army (IRA) stems from 1919, a successor to the Irish Volunteers who had staged the Easter Rising three years earlier. In fact, the name had first been used in the American Civil War of the 1860s, when the American Fenians (Republicans) formed a paramilitary force to fight in that conflict. The American interest and connection with Irish Republicanism has continued strongly to this day, but the IRA as an active organisation in Ireland itself was a twentieth-century creation.

Within the Republican movement, there has been a division since the Easter Rising, which was mounted to form a self-governing Republic of Ireland, but failed. Michael Collins led one contingent of Republicans who believed that, to achieve an independent Ireland in some form, some compromise would have to be reached with the British. The whole of Ireland was made up of 26 counties, but the 6 counties of the north, which make up Ulster, were largely pro-British. Collins was prepared to accede those 6 counties to the British to form Northern Ireland, while the other 20 became the Republic of Ireland when he signed the 1921 Anglo-Irish Treaty. However, this angered another contingent of Republicanism, who swore no compromise, and Collins was soon ambushed and assassinated by them. But the Anglo-Irish Treaty was allowed to stand as the majority of those living in Ulster's six counties wanted to stay British.

As the BBC's World Affairs correspondent Paul Reynolds pointed out, the IRA never disbanded. Their next significant action was a bombing campaign in mainland Britain at the outset of the Second World War in 1939–40, involving 127 incidents. However, the world conflict soon overshadowed any effect the campaign might have had. In the post-war years, the IRA focused on Northern Ireland, launching a 'border campaign' from 1956 to 1962, but this also achieved little.

The original IRA was being slowly superseded by a new order. The fiftieth anniversary of the Easter Rising in 1966 saw the first rumblings of the new order and the dawn of the Troubles in 1968–9 that saw a more efficient and ruthless IRA at work: the Provisional IRA, also known as the 'Provisionals' or 'Provos'. Confusingly, the general public has continued to use the name 'IRA', but the direction of this new outgrowth of the mother organisation offered no compromise, and wanted Britain out of Ireland completely and for good. The 'war' or 'terrorist atrocities' (depending on your point of view) carried out by the Provisionals was a long and bloody one lasting 30 years until the signing of the Good Friday Agreement in 1998. Gerry Adams, Leader of the Republican political wing Sinn Fein, and his deputy Martin McGuinness (who himself has admitted being a former IRA commander), reached for a compromise. There was never going to be a winner, with the IRA pitted against not only the British security forces, but also the Loyalist paramilitaries, who were fighting a brutal guerrilla campaign just like the IRA.

However, the Provisionals had also bred offshoots unwilling to compromise, including the Real IRA, the Continuity IRA and the Irish National Liberation Army (INLA). Some of these offshoots are still active today and, in 2009, there was the already mentioned Massereene Barracks Shooting and the shooting of policemen and other much smaller splinter activities up to the time of writing in late 2010. Rosemary Nelson had clients who were at least sympathetic and allegedly had links to the Provisional IRA and its offshoots, and this did not endear her to the security forces or the Loyalists.

THE UVF AND OTHER LOYALIST PARAMILITARIES

The UVF, as its name suggests, was the chief Loyalist paramilitary organisation during the Troubles, but like the IRA it would produce offshoots. It was set up as a response to the IRA, but was founded in May 1966, before the Provisional IRA began its most active campaign. It was named after the Ulster Volunteers, formed in 1912, although the connection ends there. The raison d'être of the UVF was to 'destroy all Republican paramilitary groups'. As Peter Taylor's 1999 book *Loyalists* shows, a statement of intent made on 21 May 1966 by the UVF could not have been clearer:

'From this day, we declare war against the Irish Republican Army and its splinter groups. Known IRA men will be executed mercilessly and without hesitation. Less extreme measures will be taken against sheltering or helping them, but if they persist in giving them aid, then more extreme methods will be adopted... we solemnly warn the authorities to make no more speeches of appeasement. We are heavily armed Protestants dedicated to this cause.'

Just two weeks before this statement, a group of Loyalists had petrol-bombed a Catholic pub on the Shankill Road in Belfast, and also managed accidentally to kill a Protestant widow living next door. It should always be remembered, however, that the IRA was also beginning to target civilians and carry out such atrocities and the 'tit-for-tat' mentality of the Troubles was soon a reality. But Peter Taylor's book *Loyalists* also shows that the reality of the UVF was different to the above mission statement: in the late Sixties, if they couldn't find an IRA member to target, or missed their target, they would sometimes murder a Catholic civilian instead. This was the true terror of the Troubles on both sides; murders were often random and only because of the religious persuasion of the victim, although the real targeting was, of course, political. As the academic Dr John Patrick Maher told the authors, sometimes a relationship or friendship with somebody from the other side of the divide was enough. There were instances, for example, of scalping young women because they had a boyfriend who was on the other side of the religious/political divide.

Just as space does not allow us to go into detail about the Republican outrages of the Troubles, the same goes for the Loyalists. But, during the 30-year period, two operations carried out by the UVF had high death tolls. The planting of a time bomb in McGurk's Bar, a Catholic pub, in Belfast on 4 December 1971 killed 15 people. The UVF were also to be active in the Republic, and the double operations of 17 May 1974 in Dublin and Monaghan of four car bombs killed a total of 33 and injured 300.

As we will see, in the mid-1990s there was a breakaway group formed called the LVF, and this organisation is central to Rosemary Nelson's story. Other smaller offshoots of the UVF and LVF were the Red Hand Commando and the Red Hand Defenders. The UVF declared a ceasefire in 1994, but random attacks continued until the organisation officially declared its

34

armed campaign at an end in May 2007, exactly 31 years after it had begun.

During the Troubles, for every alleged paramilitary member suspected of terrorist activity, a lawyer was needed to represent them. This proved to be a highly dangerous position for a lawyer to take.

THE KILLING OF PAT FINUCANE

When the lawyer Pat Finucane was gunned down in front of his family on 12 February 1989, he was yet another victim of the Troubles, although higher profile locally than many, having often been seen interviewed on the television news and in newspapers. He represented clients from both the Catholic and Protestant communities, but the fact that clients of his were members of the Provisionals and INLA made Pat Finucane a controversial figure to some, and a target for a few.

There is no doubt that Pat Finucane's own family had had strong links to the Provisional IRA in the past. His brother John was a member of the Provisionals and was killed in a car crash on the Falls Road in Belfast back in 1972, apparently while on 'active service'. His other brother Seamus was engaged to Mairead Farrell, one of the three IRA suspects killed by the SAS on Gibraltar in 1988. In 1976, Seamus had been arrested with the future hunger-striker Bobby Sands and seven other Provisional IRA members when they were trying to destroy a South Belfast furniture shop. Seamus was sentenced to 14 years. Prior to this, Seamus had been the leader of an IRA unit in West Belfast. Another brother, Dermot, fought and blocked extradition from the Republic to Northern Ireland for his alleged involvement in the murder of a prison officer and, in 1983, escaped from the Maze Prison with 37 other prisoners.

Bobby Sands was Pat Finucane's best-known client until his death on hunger strike in the Maze Prison in 1981, but Finucane would continue to raise his cause and also represented other IRA and INLA members who died in that protest. Other high-profile clients included Brian Gillen, a former member of the Provisionals and the IRA Army Council. Another client was Gervaise McKerr, whose husband had been shot in 1982 along with two others by the RUC, then pursuing a 'shoot-to-kill' policy.

The IRA bomber Pat McGeown (also a participant in the 1981 hunger strike, and heart disease stemming from that would later lead to his early death) was also a client, and he was charged with the organisation of the murder of two British Army corporals in 1988. Finucane argued robustly in court that there was 'insufficient evidence' against McGeown and, in November 1988, the charges were dropped. In their moment of victory, McGeown and Finucane were photographed outside the court, and this picture made the newspapers. Many believe that this was the spur for Finucane's murder just three months later.

Pat Finucane obviously had family links with the Republican paramilitaries and represented some of the members of those organisations and those associated with members. But shortly after Finucane's murder in 1989, the UDA and the UFF claimed responsibility for the killing, giving the reason that he was a high-ranking officer in the IRA himself. At Finucane's inquest, the RUC said that there was no evidence to support this accusation, and Finucane's family also strongly repudiated this.

In an article in the *Telegraph* on 18 April 2003, the IRA informer Sean O'Callaghan said that he was present at an IRA finance meeting in 1980, and that both the Sinn Fein Leader Gerry Adams and Pat Finucane were present at the meeting. Adams has strongly denied this and that he was ever a member of the IRA. Finucane had also always denied that he was an IRA member. Other senior Republicans questioned the veracity of O'Callaghan's allegations. This was added to the RUC's denial of Finucane's IRA membership.

The Stevens Inquiry into Finucane's murder (undertaken by Sir John Stevens, then Deputy-Commissioner of the Metropolitan Police and published in April 2003) uncovered evidence that led to the arrest of William Stobie, a member of the UDA for the murder of Finucane. This charge was later dropped, and Stobie was charged with 'aiding and abetting' the murder by supplying the gun, which was owned by the UDA. But Stobie's trial would break down when a key witness failed to appear (although the Loyalist group the Red Hand Defenders would later execute him). Stobie had also been involved in the murder of a 19-year-old Protestant student called Brian Lambert in 1987, who was mistaken for being a Catholic.

In his overview at the end of the Stevens Report, Sir John Stevens wrote, 'I have uncovered enough evidence to lead me to believe that the murders of Patrick Finucane and Brian Adam Lambert could have been prevented.' He also concluded that there had been collusion in Finucane's murder 'between members of the security forces, especially the Force Research Unit (FRU) and Loyalists'.

Shortly before Finucane was murdered, the Conservative Minister Douglas Hogg had stated before a House of Commons committee that some solicitors in Northern Ireland were too sympathetic towards the IRA. This had led to the Social Democratic and Labour Party (SDLP) MP Seamus Mallon warning that such statements could lead to the murder of lawyers in Northern Ireland. There was also an allegation later made by the British undercover agent Brian Nelson that he had warned the RUC that Finucane was going to be shot, but that the information was never relayed.

In September 2004, a UDA informer called Ken Barrett pleaded guilty to the murder of Pat Finucane. He was given life and told that he would serve at least 22 years. Incredibly, he was released less than two years later from Maghaberry Prison in May 2006 (although he had served almost three years in total), after a decision by the Sentence Review Commission, although his release was opposed by the then Northern Ireland Secretary Peter Hain.

Pat Finucane's son Michael was philosophical and made a statement: 'The prosecution of individuals was never a primary focus for my family. We always felt that the murder of Pat Finucane went far beyond the killing of just one man.'

3

THE BUILD-UP

Rosemary Nelson began representing political clients, both Republican and Loyalist, in the mid-1990s, but it was at the beginning of 1997 that she began to really hit the headlines, her professional actions making her a high-profile lawyer. A pressure cooker of tensions was building, as she campaigned for human rights on behalf of her clients, but she continued to follow her path, despite ominous threats and warnings. Only a member of the legal profession could truly understand her zeal and quest for justice. The law was her vocation and she gave her heart and soul for her clients.

In December 1996, the Lawyers Committee for Human Rights issued a report entitled *At the Crossroads: Human Rights and the Northern Ireland Peace Process*, and this included a directive to the British Government. It said that the British Government should 'require vigorous and independent investigation of all threats to legal counsel in Northern Ireland. Solicitors who report threats of violence should be accorded effective protection.' The murder of Finucane in February 1989 had been the first of a legal counsel in the Troubles, but this new recommendation from a respected body showed that the threat of violence against those lawyers defending clients from either side of the sectarian divide was still very much alive and real.

On 7 March 1997, Rosemary gave an interview to the New York organisation Human Rights Watch in which she made allegations that were shocking and controversial. Some of her clients who had recently been released from Gough Barracks in Armagh had told her about death threats made to them by detectives interviewing them, and also threats made against Rosemary herself through those clients. Reportedly, there were derogatory and demeaning sexual comments made about her, too, but the most chilling were the threats against her safety. With a husband and three young children, this must have been extremely worrying for her, especially with the vivid memory of fellow defence lawyer Pat Finucane's murder after receiving similar threats eight years earlier.

In the interview, Rosemary explained the nature of the alleged threats. She said that detectives had informed her clients in no uncertain terms that her personal details and photograph would be passed on to Loyalists.

Seven weeks later, on 27 April, Robert Hamill was beaten to death by a Loyalist mob and Rosemary began to represent his family. When Hamill died on 8 May, Rosemary made a public announcement that she was going to instigate legal action against the RUC for its failure to protect Hamill and his friends. She also stated that she would get access to the recorded videos from CCTV cameras overlooking the scene that night. In fact, less than two years later, Rosemary would tell the Pat Finucane Centre that the RUC had denied her access to those tapes. The alleged threats that she had reported to Human Rights Watch at the beginning of March that year had only spurred her on to see justice done, in spite of the dangers that she faced.

Two months on from that statement, Rosemary was there when the Orange Order march went down the Garvaghy Road, despite much protest from the GRRC whom Rosemary also represented. The RUC had begun to take action at the march, and Rosemary went up to RUC officers and told them that she was the GRRC's lawyer. She then asked to speak to the officer in command. An RUC officer then allegedly assaulted her, bruising her arm and shoulder, while shouting sectarian abuse at her. Rosemary said that she immediately asked for the name of the officer who attacked her, that they were not wearing identification numbers on their uniforms. She said that the RUC officers were not co-operative, allegedly telling her to 'Fuck off!' All of these allegations were subsequently strenuously denied by the RUC.

In the autumn of that year, the United Nations began to get involved in the allegations that death threats were being made to lawyers in Northern Ireland, largely a response to Rosemary's interview with Human Rights Watch earlier that year. In the last 11 days of October 1997, the UN's Special Rapporteur, Param Cumaraswamy, gathered facts to investigate those allegations. This was ostensibly focused on the alleged threats and intimidation meted out by the RUC to defence lawyers. During the investigation, Rosemary gave evidence to Mr Cumaraswamy on 24 October. In his final report, the UN Special Rapporteur wrote: 'There have been consistent reports of alleged systematic abuse of defence lawyers in Northern Ireland by certain RUC officers since 1992.' This was a very high-profile report of a pattern of alleged RUC threats towards lawyers from a leading world human rights organisation.

The UN report had contained the names of the lawyers who had made allegations about the RUC threats towards them and, of course, Rosemary Nelson's name was among them. But, before it was published, a draft copy had been sent to the Chief Constable of the RUC, Sir Ronnie Flanagan, for his perusal. Flanagan would deny making a claim in the report, directly quoted from him. He had said that allegations of RUC intimidation were part of a political agenda to show the RUC as part of the unionist (Loyalist) tradition. He was also quoted as saying that defence lawyers representing sectarian clients were passing the message to their clients to stay silent during interrogation, which the paramilitaries approved of. When Flanagan denied making both claims, the notes of the United Nations assistant who had interviewed him were checked, and were consistent with his claims. Flanagan then said that he could not guarantee the safety of the lawyers who had given evidence. Therefore, the names of all the defence lawyers, including Rosemary's, were removed from the published version of the report.

Later that year, after complaints made by Rosemary to the ICPC, the ICPC began an investigation into her claims of the death threat allegedly coming from officers within the RUC and told to her by her clients. However, just as in the case of the ICPC investigation into the murder of Robert Hamill, the RUC conducted the investigation on the ground. In consequence, RUC officers were investigating allegations made against other RUC officers. This hardly inspired confidence, but the actions of Rosemary Nelson throughout 1997 had definitely brought the allegations of RUC harassment and threats against her (and therefore other lawyers) into the open and into the media.

While Rosemary Nelson was going about her legal duties and becoming increasingly high profile, the Troubles were still being played out around her. The Loyalist paramilitary group the UVF had been going through changes itself, and one man illustrates these developments more than any other: Billy Wright. Known by the media as 'King Rat', Wright's story is linked with Rosemary Nelson's through circumstances. His activities and subsequent death had significant repercussions on Rosemary Nelson's life.

In fact, Billy Wright was not born in Northern Ireland at all, although his parents were Irish Protestants (it should be noted that they were in no way Loyalist radicals). He was born on 7 July 1960 in Wolverhampton in the West Midlands of England, when Rosemary was almost two years old in Lurgan. When he was very young, his parents moved to Mountnorris in South Armagh, a largely Catholic Nationalist area. But when he was six, Billy's parents separated and he was taken in by a children's home for a while. Young Billy was not segregated from Catholics as a child, and played freely with them, getting on well and playing Gaelic football with them. However, this would not last. By his mid-teens, Billy was turning towards his own community more and more.

In 1976, when he was approaching 16, an event happened which pushed him further in that direction. The Republicans massacred ten Protestants travelling on a bus in Kingsmill in Wright's area. In Tony Harnden's book *Bandit Country*, Wright is quoted about his reaction to this multiple murder: 'I was 15 when those workmen were pulled out of that bus and shot dead. I was a Protestant and I realised that they had been killed simply because they were Protestants. I left Mountnorris, came back to Portadown and immediately joined the youth wing of the UVF. I felt it was my duty to help my people and that is what I have been doing ever since.'

Wright said this years later when he had become a very prominent Loyalist player, and the sentiments reflect a motivation for 'going sectarian' that were echoed around Northern Ireland in the 1970s, the height of the Troubles. But while the initial motives for joining a paramilitary group were pure, to help your community and defend it against attack, and to counter-attack, as time went on less virtuous motives began to creep into such organisations. It is also unlikely that the Kingsmill massacre was the only reason for Wright joining the UVF in 1976. Founded ten years earlier in 1966 as a response to the IRA, which was reorganising as the Provisional IRA, it is enlightening that the UVF carried out the very first killing of the Troubles in the year of their formation. It is likely that Wright was already moving towards the UVF before Kingsmill, but that the massacre was the trigger for his actual joining of it.

As Rosie Cowan reported in the *Guardian* on 27 December 2000, many people who knew the young Wright said that he was indoctrinated and radicalised by Loyalist paramilitaries. It was not long before Wright was in trouble for his actions on behalf of the UVF, however. Just a year later, in 1977, he was given six years in prison for hijacking and arms offences. He served three-and-a-half years of his sentence in Crumlin Road Prison and the Maze Prison, before being released. Upon release, Wright spent a short period in Scotland, but soon returned to Portadown, close to Rosemary Nelson's hometown of Lurgan, and not far from Queen's University, Belfast, where Rosemary was graduating in law at about that time. Portadown would also be the location of one of Rosemary's most controversial cases, the Drumcree Conflict, and her representation of the GRRC.

Back in Portadown, Wright went 'straight', became an insurance salesman, married and had two daughters. In fact, he would not go back to his UVF activities for five years. More surprisingly, he also became a born-again Christian and worked as a gospel preacher in Armagh to spread the message. For a man who would lead an increasingly violent life, this strong connection to Christ and God seems perverse, going against the Christian teachings of peace and turning the other cheek. This was a contradiction not lost on Wright himself later. Quoted in Martin Dillon's *God and the Gun: The Church and Irish Terrorism*, Wright explained how he felt about this: 'You can't glorify God and seek to glorify Ulster because the challenges which are needed are paramilitary. That's a contradiction to the life God would want you to lead.'

But Wright went on to say that, while he had lapsed and was not 'walking with God', he hoped that one day God would allow him to do this again. It is obvious that Wright's allegiance to the Loyalist cause became stronger than his Christian faith, but he kept believing, although we will see that his activities would become far more than a crusader for his people.

When Wright returned to active service with the UVF in the mid-1980s, he was soon plunged into a campaign of violence. For the rest of that decade, he would be arrested again and again under suspicion of murder and conspiracy to murder. Wright became commander of the UVF Mid-Ulster brigade, a senior position in the organisation, although he was also a political militant within it. According to the security services of Northern Ireland, he directed up to 20 sectarian murders, but he was never convicted of any of them. The majority of the killings carried out by Wright's UVF unit were of Catholic civilians, but some were Republican paramilitaries. For instance, in Cappagh, County Tyrone, in 1991, the unit killed three IRA members, as well as an elderly passer-by. Wright then increasingly became an assassination target for the Provisional IRA and the INLA commanded by Dominic McGlinchley. There would be five attempts on Wright's life by the IRA, one of them a car bomb, but Wright escaped each time. But it would be the INLA that had the last word.

Wright's UVF unit gave themselves the name the 'Brat Pack', perhaps after the group of young actors famous in Hollywood in the mid-1980s. But Martin O'Hagan, a journalist for the Northern Ireland tabloid the *Sunday World*, called them the 'Rat Pack' in his articles, a name reminiscent of the group surrounding Frank Sinatra in the 1950s and '60s. But O'Hagan was not bestowing any glamour on Wright's unit, but alluding to the dirtiness of rats. Wright was reportedly annoyed by O'Hagan's swipe, especially when the name 'Rat Pack' became common currency in the Irish media and among the public, and particularly O'Hagan's naming Wright 'King Rat'. This moniker would be used in numerous headlines and tabloid media references to Wright, a fact that deeply rankled with him.

Wright could not let this go unpunished. His unit bombed the *Sunday World* offices and issued death threats to O'Hagan and all of the newspaper employees. The threat against O'Hagan would not be carried out by Wright, but would be later by Loyalists. But it is unlikely that O'Hagan was killed for his satirical name-calling, although this brought him to the attention of the UVF in the first place. It was O'Hagan's crusading journalism against the alleged drugs-racket activities of Loyalist gangs that did for him. This even murkier side to Wright and his activities cannot be overlooked here.

A report in the *Guardian* on 17 November 2001 claimed that Wright had been one of the largest drug-dealers in the Mid-Ulster area, specifically of the drug Ecstasy. Martin O'Hagan investigated these links and the alleged drug links of Wright's successors.

In 2010, Ed Moloney published a book, *Voices from the Grave: Two Men's War in Ireland*, that has some enlightening views on Wright from somebody who knew the situation on the ground. The book is focused on two interviews with former IRA commander Brendan 'The Dark' Hughes and David Ervine, the former outspoken leader of the Progressive Unionist Party (PUP). Ervine was a former UVF member himself; he was arrested for possession of explosives and the threat to endanger life in 1974, and sentenced to 11 years in the Maze Prison, but was released in 1980. Both men gave interviews to Moloney on the understanding that they would not be published until they had died. David Ervine died in 2007 and Hughes a year later, so Moloney was finally able to publish his book.

Claims made by Brendan Hughes in the book are controversial in themselves, as he alleges that Gerry Adams, the Sinn Fein leader, was a pivotal figure in IRA policy, specifically stopping the public execution of IRA informers, but sending them into 'hiding' (a euphemism for being killed and disposed of). Adams has always firmly denied being an IRA member, and so would obviously robustly refute such claims. The views of David Ervine are very interesting about Billy Wright. In the interview, Ervine claimed that Wright was 'heavily involved with drugs' and gave a specific example. Ervine says, 'There was a notorious story about a dance hall in Northern Ireland, where, on one side of the hall, the Irish National Liberation Army (INLA) sold certain types of drugs and, on the other side, Billy Wright's UVF members sold a different type of drugs.' Ervine went on to say that the INLA and Wright had 'carved up' the drugs market. This is incredible, as both sides were violent sectarian enemies, with a mortal hatred of each other, and lends credence to the drug-racket allegations involving both sectarian sides in Northern Ireland.

In October 1994, the UVF leadership and other Loyalist paramilitaries called for a ceasefire. Billy Wright was vehemently opposed to this cessation of the armed struggle, and began to break away from the UVF leadership's control. It was the Drumcree Conflict – the disputed Orange Order march down the Garvaghy Road in Portadown (the heart of Wright's territory) – which really got his blood up. Rosemary Nelson was very actively involved in this conflict, representing over 200 members of the GRRC. The UVF leaders did nothing to protest against this perceived Catholic/Republican victory, either verbally or violently. This was when Wright began actively to order killings on his own with no UVF direction.

On 9 July 1996, the body of a Catholic taxi-driver, Michael McGoldrick, was found in his taxi in a small lane near Lurgan, Rosemary Nelson's hometown. He had picked up a fare in Lurgan the day before, and had been shot five times in the head. A few years later, a former Loyalist supergrass, Clifford McKeown, was sentenced to 24 years for McGoldrick's murder. McKeown claimed that it was a birthday present for Billy Wright (Wright had turned 36 the day before McGoldrick picked up McKeown).

Largely as a result of this rogue killing which broke the ceasefire (in addition to Wright's public verbal attacks on the UVF leadership), Wright was thrown out of the UVF on 2 August 1996 when his UVF unit was 'stood down'. He was also threatened with execution by the organisation. Wright appeared at the Drumcree standoff and made a public statement: 'I will not be leaving Ulster, I will not change my mind about what I believe is happening in Ulster. But all I would like to say is that it has broken my heart to think that fellow Loyalists would turn their guns on me, and I have to ask them, "For whom are you doing it?"' But, despite this plea, Wright was a strong-minded and hardened man, and paid the threat no notice.

According to Susan McKay's book *Northern Protestants: An Unsettled People*, it was at Drumcree that Wright's brigade smuggled homemade weapons in, allegedly with no resistance from members of the Orange Order. In his book *The Troubles: Ireland's Ordeal*, Tim Coogan alleges that Wright's UVF unit planned to drive petrol tankers into Catholic/Nationalist housing estates and explode them. In that same month of August 1996, Wright showed his true disregard for the UVF by forming his breakaway LVF.

It is important here to emphasise the huge charisma that Wright possessed. He had the ability to inspire not just sectarian Loyalist passion, but also loyalty to himself. The effect he had on Mark Fulton, who effectively became Wright's second-in-command and later leader of the LVF, was very powerful. In this way, he managed to take his UVF unit with him into the LVF, and, when other disaffected Loyalists joined, it was estimated that the LVF had a maximum strength of around 250 members, a formidable force. The LVF would remain active until 2005 and, under Wright's leadership, the killings of five people were attributed to the LVF (although they were not formally claimed), including the taxi-driver Michael McGoldrick and a Catholic woman sleeping in the bed of her Protestant boyfriend. They also tortured a Catholic man and beat him to death with a hammer, before setting his body alight. Two more taxi-drivers were targeted, but escaped when the gun jammed on both occasions, one of them in Lurgan. Added to this, there were bombs planted in Dundalk in the Republic, but the Gardai defused the bombs on both occasions. In June 1997, Mo Mowlam, then Secretary of State for Northern Ireland, made the LVF officially illegal.

A month later, the body of a Catholic civilian, James Morgan, was found. Aged just 16, he was found in a pit meant for animal remains close to the village of Clough in South Down. In January 1999, LVF member Norman Coopey was convicted of Morgan's murder and sentenced to life, but was released 18 months later under the terms of the Good Friday Agreement.

So Billy Wright's Loyalist splinter paramilitary group the LVF was active and taking no prisoners. In March 1997, Billy Wright was finally convicted of threatening to kill a woman, given eight years, and was initially imprisoned in HMP Maghaberry, but was sent to the Maze Prison a month later. In May 1997, the LVF signed up to a ceasefire, ostensibly to get an early release for Wright and other imprisoned members. Meanwhile, Wright's demands for a place for 26 fellow inmates and himself in the LVF section of the prison were granted. Although threatened with execution by fellow Loyalists, Wright was shrewd enough to know where the gravest danger to him lay.

The Maze Prison, in Lisburn near Belfast, was the main high-security holding prison for paramilitary prisoners in Northern Ireland between August 1971 and September 2000. It gained legendary status after the Republican hunger strikes carried out by Bobby Sands and his associates in 1981. Known locally as 'Long Kesh' or 'the

H Blocks', the latter name derived from the structure of the prison. Those convicted of terrorist offences after 1 March 1976 were held in eight 'H'-shaped blocks. By the time that Billy Wright was sent there in 1997, the H Blocks were segregated into sectarian sections, obviously to prevent violence and retaliation. INLA inmates were held in the A and B Wings of H Block 6 and LVF prisoners in C and D wings, where Wright was housed.

Wright had not been there long when LVF prisoners rioted over their visiting rooms in August 1997, and tensions began to build in the prison. Reportedly, the INLA prisoners informed staff that they would attack the LVF inmates if they could. Prison officers had serious concerns about these threats and, in response, the Prison Officers Association announced that measures had been taken to stop LVF and INLA prisoners ever coming into contact. Incredibly, within a few months that is just what happened.

On the morning of 27 December 1997, Billy Wright and another LVF prisoner were being transported in a white prison van to another part of the prison, the visiting centre. Inside the van (apart from the driver) were two guards with the prisoners. The van never reached its destination. Three INLA volunteers and fellow prisoners – John Glennon, John Kennaway and Christopher 'Crip' McWilliams – armed with two pistols between them, pushed through a pre-cut hole in a fence. Billy Wright never stood a chance. Kennaway took the driver hostage, while Glennon made sure that Wright and his companion did not escape once the side door of the van had been opened. McWilliams fired four rounds into Wright with his PA63 pistol, killing him.

Once the shooting was over, the three INLA men calmly gave themselves up to prison guards. They also gave a statement: 'Billy Wright was executed for one reason and one reason only, and that was for directing and waging his campaign from his prison cell in Long Kesh.'

The fact that Wright had been killed in a maximum-security prison, where extra precautions had been taken after threats had been made against the LVF, led to many believing that the authorities had colluded with the INLA to have Wright killed. The reason for this was that he was seen as a major thorn in the side of the developing peace process, with the Good Friday Agreement just months away. This was a reverse allegation of collusion against the authorities: the cases of Rosemary Nelson, Pat Finucane, Robert Hamill and others would give rise to claims of alleged collusion between the Loyalists and the Northern Ireland security forces, while this was allegedly between the Republicans and those same authorities. A public inquiry into Wright's death opened in May 2007 under Lord Maclean.

On 14 September 2010, the *Billy Wright Inquiry Report* that had cost £30m was finally published. It found that there had been no collusion between the prison authorities, police and security services, but there had been negligence of care by the Northern Ireland Prison Service. The Northern Ireland Secretary, Owen Paterson, told the British Parliament that it was 'clear and unequivocal' that there had been no collusion. The negligence arose from the decision to move Wright to the H Block of the Maze. Paterson said, 'Specifically, the panel finds that "the decision to allocate Billy Wright and the LVF faction to H Block 6 in April 1997 alongside the

INLA prisoners was a wrongful act that directly facilitated his murder..." I am sincerely sorry that failings in the system facilitated his murder.'

The report also laid some blame at the feet of the RUC for failing to communicate a key piece of information, citing that it was 'a wrongful omission'. It was also critical of the PSNI (which replaced the RUC) for being 'slow and reluctant' in providing information, and which had given the inquiry its 'greatest difficulties'. It concluded that, while some of this was due to failures of police information-management systems, there was a suspicion that there had been 'deliberate malpractice', including destroying audit trails and not being forthcoming with evidence.

The British domestic security service MI5 was also not left unscathed; the report concluded that it was 'most unfortunate' that the intelligence about a death threat to Wright had not been passed on by MI5 to Adam Ingram, the Security Minister at the time. The report did, however, recommend that a commission should be set up to investigate the Northern Ireland Prison Service.

Was it negligence or collusion? Why was Wright moved into H Block 6 of the Maze from Maghaberry Prison despite INLA death threats? How did the INLA prisoners get the guns? How were they (or somebody else) able to cut a hole in a fence beforehand in preparation for the hit? How did they know that Wright would be in the van at that time and on that day? There are still very serious questions that need answers, after a very expensive 'independent' public inquiry taking years.

The man who pulled the trigger on Billy Wright, John McWilliams, died of cancer before he could give evidence to the inquiry. But in 2000, he gave an interview to the BBC's *Newsnight* about the prison authorities and police. McWilliams said, 'They had warnings for three or four months. So obviously they turned a blind eye to it.' The father of Billy Wright, David Wright, called the inquiry report 'a whitewash'.

Retribution for Wright's murder happened very swiftly. That very night of 27 December 1997, the LVF targeted the largely Catholic/Nationalist area of Dungannon by opening fire in a disco, killing a Provisional IRA volunteer and wounding four civilians. As reported in the *Scotsman* on 31 January 1998, just over a month after Wright's murder, the Loyalists warned that there would be a 'measured military response' to Wright's murder. In fact, the LVF moved closer to another Loyalist paramilitary group, the UFF, under the leadership of the equally powerful and charismatic Johnny 'Mad Dog' Adair. The later murder of the journalist Martin O'Hagan in 2001 can be linked to Billy Wright and, as we shall see later, it had significant repercussions for Rosemary Nelson.

Billy Wright swiftly became a martyr for hardcore Loyalists and his influence was almost as strong as when he was alive. As reported in the *Guardian* on 17 November 2001, paramilitaries in Portadown in 2000 told journalists, 'He did what he had to do to ensure that our faith and culture were kept intact.' The impact of his charismatic leadership still remains today, and Wright's influence is still felt acutely in the form of his successor as leader of the LVF, Mark Fulton.

A fortnight after Wright's murder, Rosemary Nelson was still trying to highlight alleged human rights injustices linked to the security forces in Northern Ireland. Along with 32 other lawyers (including Barra McGrory, who represents the Nelson family today), she signed a petition, issued as a statement: 'We, the undersigned members of the legal profession in Northern Ireland, wish to express our grave concern at the failure of the rule of law and the relative immunity from prosecution of members of the security forces who have violated basic human rights and contravened national and international laws.' This was the main thrust of Rosemary Nelson's human rights crusade, as she saw injustice all around her. The statement continued: 'It is a fundamental tenet of the rule of law that all are subject equally to the law and that no one is above the law. Yet in our professional experience we have witnessed numerous incidents where this basic principle has been abandoned.'

But the statement also focused on the murder of the lawyer Pat Finucane nine years earlier, too. It read: 'We remain particularly concerned at the circumstances of the murder of our esteemed professional colleague, Pat Finucane. It is simply unacceptable that faced with compelling evidence of State involvement in the killing of a defence lawyer, no action has been taken. Serious allegations of collusion between members of illegal Loyalist organisations and members of the security forces have yet to be properly investigated.' Finucane's case was still firmly in everybody's memory, especially as he had been a defence lawyer just like the signatories of the petition.

The alleged threats made to lawyers by RUC officers were also covered. We know that Rosemary Nelson herself had allegedly received such threats through her clients from members of the RUC. 'Similarly, no action has been taken about the continuing intimidation and abuse of solicitors by police officers via their clients in detention centres. We are all too aware of this continuing problem, which is one we face in our daily lives.' A Law Society of England and Wales report was then quoted about the alleged threats and the reporting of them: 'There have been persistent reports that RUC CID officers interrogating detainees in the holding centres routinely disparage and make threats against particular solicitors.' (The end of the statement called for the abolition of the detention centres where their clients were held.)

This was then supported by the fact that the UN Special Rapporteur on the Independence of Judges and Lawyers had been in Northern Ireland several months earlier investigating these claims. The following day, 15 January 1998, in a *Dispatches* documentary broadcast on Channel 4, the UN Special Rapporteur himself, Param Cumaraswamy, appeared and voiced his particular concern regarding Rosemary Nelson's safety. This was the first mainstream official broadcast made by a highly respected and impartial UN representative and so was very important in highlighting the dangers facing Nelson.

Rosemary Nelson herself continued to be highly visible, going about her professional duties representing her clients. In February, she said she felt 'outrage' at the arrest of the brother of Robert Hamill (who had been beaten to death by a Loyalist mob a year earlier). His brother was pulled in for questioning about disturbances along the Garvaghy Road, recently at the centre of the Drumcree Conflict. Rosemary was acting as the lawyer for Robert Hamill's family, and saw his brother's arrest as harassment.

In March 1998, the report made by the UN Special Rapporteur Param Cumaraswamy was published. It was direct in its language. He reached the conclusion that 'the RUC has engaged in activities which constitute intimidation, hindrance, harassment or improper interference' and that 'the RUC has identified solicitors with their clients or their clients' causes as a result of discharging their functions'.

It was at this time that Rosemary Nelson allegedly received a new veiled threat. One of her clients, who had spent seven days being questioned in Castlereagh, is said to have told Rosemary that RUC CID officers made obscene and offensive remarks about her. But the really chilling allegation by one of her clients is that an RUC officer purportedly said that a law had been passed in 1989 to deal with solicitors aiding their clients. The client later told the *Irish News* that Rosemary Nelson had told him that no such law existed in the statutes. But then she became frightened when it dawned on her that 'the 1989 law' was allegedly a reference to the murder of her fellow defence lawyer Pat Finucane in that year.

In May, Rosemary Nelson was back in the news protesting at the fact that it had been decided not to hold an inquest into the murder of Sam Marshall in Armagh in 1990 (Marshall was murdered when leaving an RUC station with Rosemary's client Colin Duffy and another man). As we have seen, there were allegations of RUC collusion in the murder.

July 1998 was a busy one for Rosemary Nelson. On 18 July, she attended a meeting between the British Prime Minister Tony Blair's Chief of Staff Jonathan Powell and her clients, the GRRC, who had recently been embroiled in the Drumcree Conflict, but there were still unresolved tensions. At the meeting, the problem of personal security of the members of the meeting was brought up. The alleged threats against Rosemary Nelson would have been a key part of these discussions. Three days later, another meeting with Jonathan Powell saw more talk about personal security. A leaflet was then doing the rounds in Portadown that threatened the personal safety of Rosemary Nelson and Breandan Mac Cionnaith, a politician and then the spokesman for the GRRC. He had gone to prison for six years for involvement in the bombing of the British Legion hall in Portadown in the early 1980s.

According to the minutes of the meeting that Rosemary Nelson also attended, an RUC superintendent told Mac Cionnaith that 'all the RUC could provide was crime prevention advice'. The GRRC members expressed their frustrations about their personal security at the meeting and the 'dismissive' attitude of the RUC when responding to death threats. Two days after that, as a result of what was discussed at the last meeting, two officials from the Northern Ireland Office (NIO) met with the group to talk about security protection for the two councillors among them. But Rosemary Nelson was not included, as she was not an elected official, despite probably being in the greatest danger.

In that same month, the ICPC aired their 'serious concerns' about the RUC procedures in its own investigation into death threats made against Rosemary Nelson to the Northern Ireland Secretary Dr Mo Mowlam and Ronnie Flanagan, the Chief Constable of the RUC. As a consequence, London Metropolitan Police

Commander Niall Mulvihill was sent in to lead his own investigation into the threats, replacing the RUC.

On 29 September 1998, Rosemary Nelson addressed the US Congress in Washington DC, giving evidence to the International Operations and Human Rights Subcommittee at a hearing on human rights in Northern Ireland. As it is Rosemary Nelson's most internationally high-profile statement on the subject and her experience of it, it is worth quoting in full here. This was Rosemary Nelson's statement to the US Congress:

'I have been a solicitor in private practice in Northern Ireland for the past 12 years. My practice includes a mixture of several areas of law including crime, matrimonial and personal injury cases. My clients are drawn from both sides of the community. For the last ten years I have been representing suspects detained for questioning about politically motivated offences. All of these clients have been arrested under emergency laws and held in specially designed holding centres. There are three such centres across Northern Ireland. Since I began to represent such clients and especially since I became involved in a high-profile murder case, I have begun to experience difficulties with the RUC.

'These difficulties have involved RUC officers questioning my professional integrity, making allegations that I am a member of a paramilitary group and, at their most serious, making threats against my personal safety including death threats. All of these remarks have been made to my clients in my absence because lawyers in Northern Ireland are

routinely excluded from interviews with clients detained in the holding centres.

'This behaviour on the part of RUC officers has worsened during the last two years and particularly since I began to represent the residents of the Garvaghy Road, who have objected to an Orange Order march passing through their area from Drumcree Church. Last year I was present on the Garvaghy Road when the parade was forced through. I had been present on the road for a number of days because I had instructions from my clients to apply for an emergency judicial review of any decision allowing the parade to pass through the area. When the police began to move into the area in forces in the early hours of 5 July, I went to the police lines and identified myself as a lawyer representing the residents. I asked to speak to the officer in charge. At that point I was physically assaulted by a number of RUC officers and subjected to sectarian verbal abuse. I sustained bruising to my arm and shoulder. The officers responsible were not wearing any identification numbers and when I asked for their names I was told to 'fuck off'. I complained about the assault and abuse but to date have obtained no satisfactory response from the RUC.

'Since then my clients have reported an increasing number of incidents when I have been abused by RUC officers, including several death threats against myself and members of my family. I have also received threatening telephone calls and letters. Although I have tried to ignore these threats, inevitably I have had to take account of the possible

consequences for my family and for my staff. No lawyer in Northern Ireland can forget what happened to Patrick Finucane nor dismiss it from their minds. The allegations of official collusion in his murder are particularly disturbing and can only be resolved by an independent inquiry into his murder, as has been recommended by the UN Special Rapporteur. I would be grateful if the Subcommittee could do all in its power to bring about such an inquiry, by communicating to the United Kingdom Government its belief that an inquiry in this case would, in fact, be a boost to the peace process, as it has been in the Bloody Sunday case.

'I have also complained about these threats, again without any satisfactory response. Although complaints against the RUC are supervised by the Independent Commission for Police Complaints, the complaints themselves are investigated by RUC officers. Recently, a senior police officer from England has been called in to investigate my complaints in view of the RUC's apparent inability to handle my complaints impartially. This English police officer is interviewing witnesses himself and has decided not to rely on any assistance from the RUC.

'I believe that one of the reasons that RUC officers have been able to indulge in such systematic abuse against me is that the conditions under which they interview clients detained under emergency laws allow them to operate without sufficient scrutiny. My access to my clients can be deferred for periods of up to 48 hours. I am never allowed to be present while my clients are interviewed. Interviews are now

subject to silent video recording but are not yet being audio-recorded, although that is due to be introduced. The UN Special Rapporteur has made a number of recommendations that would remedy this situation, which to date have not been implemented. I should be grateful if this Subcommittee would lend their support to what he proposes.

'Another reason why RUC officers abuse me in this way is because they are unable to distinguish me as a professional lawyer from the alleged crimes and causes of my clients. This tendency to identify me with my clients has led to accusations by RUC officers that I have been involved in paramilitary activity, which I deeply and bitterly resent. The Special Rapporteur has recommended that RUC officers be sensitised to the important role played by defence lawyers in the criminal justice system. To date this recommendation has not been implemented. I should be grateful if this Subcommittee would ask the UK Government what steps they intend to take to act on this recommendation.

'I, like many others, was pleased to see the human rights provisions included in the recently signed Agreement. In particular, I was pleased that the Agreement looked to the early removal of the emergency provisions legislation which has been in place in some shape or form since the inception of the State. The existence of this legislation has seriously undermined public confidence in the rule of law and led to numerous miscarriages of justice, some of which have involved my clients. I was therefore very disappointed when, in the wake of the horrific

Omagh bombing, new and draconian legislation was introduced which further erodes suspects' due process rights. For example, the legislation provides for the opinion of a senior RUC officer that someone is a member of a proscribed organisation to be accepted as evidence by the courts. I and many of my colleagues fear that if these laws are used they will lead to further miscarriages of justice. Although this legislation has already been passed, I hope that the Subcommittee will express its concern to the British Government that it will not be used.

'I believe that my role as a lawyer in defending the rights of my clients is vital. The test of a new society in Northern Ireland will be to the extent to which it can recognise and respect that role, and enable me to discharge it without improper interference. I look forward to that day.'

It was an impassioned speech, and one that enhanced Rosemary Nelson's reputation as a human rights lawyer internationally, particularly in America, and that country's interest in her story would grow stronger in time. One point that had until then not been widely publicised was the fact that she had allegedly been accused by members of the RUC of 'being involved in paramilitary activity', which was basically being labelled a terrorist. Indeed, there had also been comments made by Loyalists that she had been a Republican paramilitary bomb-maker. Also, that the paralysed state of the left side of her face, the result of Rosemary's childhood operations to remove the birthmark from her face, was caused by a bomb which had exploded next to her. Verbal attacks do not come much more vicious than that.

On a visit to London on 10 December 1998, Rosemary Nelson gave an interview to *Socialist Campaign Group News*. She reiterated many of the claims she had made before the US Congress a few months earlier, but gave more details. As any good defence lawyer would do, Rosemary highlighted the injustices allegedly meted out to her own clients:

'I have represented people in politically sensitive cases for ten years. It was fine until I took on the case of Colin Duffy. He was released on appeal following the arrest in Scotland of the prosecution's key witness on charges of gun-running for Loyalist paramilitaries. Soon afterwards, uniformed RUC officers and detectives started telling people not to request Rosemary Nelson to defend them, as she would soon be dead. I lodged a complaint with the RUC – which investigates itself in such cases. The Independent Commission for Police Complaints refused to issue a certificate to say that my complaint had been properly investigated by the RUC because they had found matters of grave concern regarding the conduct of the investigation.

'In another incident, Sam Marshall was shot dead in Lurgan in 1990 just after leaving a police station to sign for bail. He had previously reported being told by an RUC detective that the next time he saw him he would be "in a body bag". In the face of accusations of collusion, the Detective Inspector conducted an investigation and exonerated himself.

It was later admitted that one of the cars that had been shadowing Marshall immediately prior to his murder was a security force surveillance vehicle. To date, the coroner has refused to conduct an inquest into Marshall's death. I am in the process of referring the case to the High Court.'

The case of Robert Hamill, beaten and kicked to death by a Loyalist mob in April 1997, was also brought up. Rosemary Nelson had represented his family. She stated:

'He had gone to a dance in the town centre. Normally Nationalists would get a taxi to cross the town through fear of attack. But as they saw an RUC Land Rover with four heavily armed officers inside, they assumed they would be safe. They were attacked by a gang of Loyalists who jumped on Robert's head shouting, "Die, Fenian, die!" One of the girls with Robert banged on the door of the Land Rover just 15 yards away and pleaded with the officers to help. They did nothing. Robert died 12 days later. No arrests were made until after his death and only one person remains in custody. The officers involved did not even make a statement about the incident when they went off duty that evening. Robert's family has shown enormous courage in campaigning for justice. As a result, they have been subjected to repeated harassment by the RUC.'

Also addressed in the interview was the situation faced by her clients, the GRRC, and specifically the Drumcree Conflict in Portadown. Rosemary Nelson said,

'Portadown is a no-go area for Nationalists. There are more than 1,000 Loyal Order parades each year. The Nationalist community is confined to a township and has been under siege by the Orange Order since last July. In 1997, the RUC moved in at 3.00am and split heads and broke limbs of the residents to force the Orange Order march down the Garvaghy Road.'

Rosemary then went on to document the abuse she had allegedly been subjected to by RUC officers herself when she approached them, something she had also told the US Congress.

The interview also turned to the alleged death threats made against Rosemary personally. 'My involvement in cases like these has made me a target for death threats and intimidation. A couple of months ago another of my clients was taken to an RUC interrogation centre and told, "Tell Rosemary we've been doing this for the last 30 years and we'll be doing it for the next 30." These threats are taken seriously.'

The interview then focused on the ubiquitous shadow of terror among Northern Ireland defence lawyers cast by the murder of Pat Finucane almost ten years earlier. Rosemary added:

'No one has ever been brought to justice for the murder of the defence lawyer Pat Finucane on 12 February 1989. That murder sent shock waves through the legal profession in Northern Ireland. The UN Special Rapporteur commented that the Northern Ireland Law Society had not been effective in combating intimidation – they did not even condemn Pat Finucane's murder. The Stevens Inquiry

looked into it. But its findings were never made public, with the result that lawyers are still afraid to take on politically sensitive cases knowing that when these people say you are going to die, they mean it.'

At the end of the interview, Rosemary made a heartfelt statement about the prejudice she felt she had suffered. 'Under the terms of the Good Friday Agreement, there has to be an ethos of human rights. But I have been shocked to find that to argue for human rights means you are classified as a Republican. In spite of thousands of complaints by the public, no RUC officer has ever been convicted of anything done while on duty. Cosmetic changes won't work. We need a new police service permeated from top to bottom by an ethos of respect for human rights.'

The beginning of the following year saw Rosemary Nelson as active as ever. On 18 January 1999, she met with the then British Prime Minister Tony Blair, accompanied by her clients, members of the GRRC. They gave the Prime Minister a report they had compiled highlighting illegal Orange Order parades in the Garvaghy Road vicinity and a logging of intimidation and threats aimed at local residents. Rosemary Nelson was by now extremely high profile and she was beginning to open high-level doors in her crusade for her clients.

Almost a month later on 12 February, she was a keynote speaker at a night organised to mark the tenth anniversary of the killing of defence lawyer Patrick Finucane at the Pat Finucane Centre in Derry. The Centre had been set up to commemorate Finucane and carry out research into sectarian intimidation and injustices and is still active today. On the same day, the *Irish Times* published a petition signed by 1,200 lawyers from around the world calling for an independent judicial inquiry into Finucane's murder. Alleged collusion by the British security forces in his death is a key focus of this call for such an inquiry with an international reach.

On 11 March, the Solicitors Criminal Bar Association, then the representative of 50 law firms, and which had represented Finucane himself, gave its support to a judicial review. The review was investigating the decision by the Law Society of Northern Ireland not to permit its Human Rights Committee to examine Finucane's murder. Actions against alleged human rights abuses and injustices, not least alleged collusion, were beginning to gain political momentum. Rosemary Nelson was a key and visible figure at the forefront of such actions.

On 15 March 1999, the *Irish News* reported that the family of Robert Hamill (who, as we have seen, was beaten to death by a Loyalist mob almost two years earlier with RUC officers present), who were represented by Rosemary Nelson, was speaking closely with the family of Stephen Lawrence in London. Stephen was a black teenager stabbed to death in an overtly racial attack in London in 1993. Rosemary Nelson was quoted in the article saying, 'He [Robert Hamill] was targeted because he was a Catholic. We are seeing racism here, racism dressed up as sectarianism.'

Also in that day's paper, a whole page was given over to an article about the RUC's alleged lack of action in dealing with illegal Loyalist activity in Portadown, an echo of the purpose of Rosemary's and the GRRC's visit to Tony Blair two months earlier. Rosemary Nelson was quoted as saying, 'Sight has been lost of the fact that there has been a legally binding decision made by the Parades Commission last year which clearly states that the Orange Order should disperse and not remain on the hill. The law has been flouted openly. We do not have "two sides equally intransigent" as is often said. We have a Nationalist community trapped, living in a village on the edge of town. It is not about conflicting rights here, it is about the law.'

That very day would prove to be the last day of Rosemary Nelson's life.

4

ALLEGED ABUSE AND DEATH THREATS

As we have seen, there were numerous threats made against Rosemary Nelson while she continued to represent her clients and grew in public stature. She was naturally very concerned about these threats, for her husband and three young children as much as for herself. But she did not crumble under this enormous pressure, but continued to press for justice, investigations into alleged human rights abuses and alleged State collusion in terrible acts of violence. To understand the true venality of the threats against her, it is important to see how they developed.

In 2004, Judge Peter Cory published a report on Rosemary Nelson (HC473, Parliamentary Copyright), the result of the Cory Collusion Inquiry into her case. It remains a prime source of evidence highlighting the dangers Rosemary faced. A full appraisal of this report is offered later.

The first threat made by telephone to Rosemary

Nelson's office in William Street, Lurgan, was received as early as late October 1993. On the day that the call was made, the girlfriend of a man known as 'Mr L' was due to see Rosemary Nelson in her office. The caller, a man, said, 'This is the UVF here... Mr L is on his way to get to your office... there'll be a black wreath there and when he gets there he'll be dead.' This threat was, of course, made against Mr L, but it is significant, as it was the first time on record of any violence threatened against anybody connected with Rosemary Nelson. The call was reported to the police (the RUC), who sent a crime-prevention officer to speak to Rosemary Nelson. This officer went to her office three times and left a letter for her there as well as crime-prevention and security leaflets on another occasion. Rosemary Nelson was supposed to get in touch with the officer, but never called him.

Judge Cory states in his report, 'I must note this early refusal by Rosemary Nelson to co-operate. It is difficult to both demand complete protection from the police force and yet deny it any co-operation.' But Cory also adds that 'an ambivalent attitude towards the RUC appears to have prevailed in the Catholic community. Some of it may have stemmed from a perception that the RUC was untrustworthy.' Judge Cory then reiterates that, if a section of the community wants the police's protection, but does not co-operate, it is 'still difficult'.

Almost three years later in September 1996, a man with a local Lurgan accent made an anonymous call to Rosemary's office. A young woman on Rosemary's staff took the call from the man who sounded 'angry'. To put it in context, on that day a man whom Cory calls 'Client A' had been released after having been arrested on suspicion of murder. The caller said, 'Have yous no conscience up there? Yous have got a murderer out of jail after killing innocent people. All Rosemary Nelson does is support IRA members. Rosemary's in the IRA herself. You are all scummy bastards... We'll get Rosemary and we'll kill her.' This call was not reported to anyone at the time.

On 2 February 1997, a man known as 'Client B' in the Cory Report was being questioned by the RUC, and asked to have his solicitor, Rosemary Nelson, present. She duly arrived but, after she left, the officers allegedly started to make insulting, personal and sectarian remarks about Rosemary, as Client B reported in a statement made on 27 October that year. Client B stated, '[They] started to fire abuse at me in relation to my solicitor. They said she was a money-grabbing bitch... as bad as Client A... she was a Provo solicitor... They also made fun of the marks on Rosemary's face... They called her a bastard fucker... They kept going on to me about Rosemary Nelson getting Client A off.'

Nine days later on 11 February 1997, the RUC arrested two men known as Client H and Client I in the Cory Report. Client H was represented by Rosemary and visited by her twice a day while he was in police custody and also had negative remarks about Rosemary directed at him when Nelson was not there. Client H said that the RUC said that Rosemary Nelson 'was a friend of the Provos and of Client A' and that she was 'not that good, she won't get you off'. Client I also reported that the RUC spoke to him about Client H and Rosemary, saying, 'He is hiding something, we need to get it out of him, the PIRA [Provisional IRA] bastard, you're dead. Tell Rosemary she's going to die, too.'

In March 1997, a man termed Client F by Cory was arrested and taken to Gough Barracks and, in a statement that Client F gave on 6 November 1997, he said that Rosemary was often referred to during his second day of questioning by the CID. Client F reported that the officers said, 'She is a terrorist with a deformed face.' And he said they asked him why he was 'seeing Rosemary' and that he was 'a game bastard as she had a face on her like a man's ball bag'.

On 25 June 1997, Client A was questioned by the RUC about murder charges. He reported that one RUC officer said to him, 'You murdered those people, I'm sure your mother and wife were proud of you and I'm sure Rosemary's very proud of you.'

Rosemary Nelson penned a letter of complaint to the Custody Sergeant at Gough Barracks about these comments, and a copy was sent to an official of British Irish Rights Watch (BIRW). As the Cory Report states, 'Client A and Rosemary Nelson took this comment to be a suggestion that Rosemary Nelson was associated with and condoned violent paramilitary activity.'

As the Cory Report also states, 'Client A was charged with the murder of two RUC officers on 23 June 1997. When it became known that Rosemary Nelson was his solicitor, the threats against her appeared to escalate.' In a statement made in October 1997 by Rosemary Nelson and referred to in the Cory Report, she outlined 'four death threats received at her home and office'. These were that a man called her office and a young woman on her staff answered the phone and she was told that 'they were nothing but IRA bastards and fuckers and that they would get Rosemary Nelson'. Another caller was put through to Rosemary Nelson directly and he said, 'You're a dead IRA fucker,' before hanging up. Subsequently, another secretary took a call in which a man said, 'You're IRA bastards and you are going to get shot.' Finally, a call was made to Rosemary Nelson's home, which was picked up by her son Christopher and, when he passed the receiver to his mother, she was told 'You're dead... you'll be shot.'

Also in October 1997, there were separate alleged incidents involving three of Rosemary's clients. Three soldiers of the Royal Irish Regiment (RIR) searched a man termed Client D. Client D reported that the soldiers made 'derogatory comments' about Rosemary Nelson several times while he was being searched. On 14 October 1997, Rosemary wrote a letter to the Chief Superintendent of the Lurgan RUC station about this incident, and she also sent a copy of the letter to BIRW.

Then there was Client G, who made a statement on 28 March 2000 regarding a visit he had made to Rosemary's William Street office on 29 October 1997. He was informed there that a friend of his son had been 'put through a window by a Royal Irish Regiment (RIR) soldier or soldiers'. Client G then walked towards a soldier, who shouted, 'I'll do the same to you,' which prompted Rosemary Nelson to go over to the soldier and say to him, 'I heard you threaten Client G.' The soldier then allegedly started to throw abuse at Rosemary, about her partially paralysed face, saying she was 'ugly' and that she was 'a Provie bastard' for getting her clients released from prison. The statement also said that the soldier told Nelson that he was going to 'nut her or do her' or some such words. A complaint was made to the

RUC about the abuse of Client G but, as the Cory Report states, it is not known if this also included the abuse directed at Rosemary Nelson.

In a statement given on 6 November 1997, Client C said that he had also been subjected to abuse about his solicitor Rosemary Nelson when arrested and taken to Gough Barracks in the previous month. Questioned by two Special Branch officers, one said that 'Rosemary must have been hit by an ugly stick about ten times', and that he was lucky that he had not been arrested at Hallowe'en 'as Rosemary would have been out on her broomstick and I wouldn't have got her down'. Client C added that about three years previously he had been asked by the police why he was represented by Rosemary as 'she does all the Provos'.

On 15 December 1997, Client E, represented by Rosemary, was arrested and, while he was in a police car with four RUC officers, one said that 'Rosemary won't help you this time', and another reportedly said, 'She won't be here that long, she'll be dead.' Again, a copy of this statement was sent to BIRW. In February 1998, Client G was arrested and taken to Castlereagh and, when he requested to see his solicitor, Rosemary was allegedly told, 'Tell prune-face that we have been doing this for 30 years and she won't be able to stop us. There was a law passed in 1989 against solicitors who concocted statements.' As recorded earlier in this book, it is alleged that Rosemary Nelson took this reference to 1989 to mean the slaying of defence lawyer Patrick Finucane but, as BIRW highlighted in a memo, this could have referred to legislation passed in that year which reduced the right to silence. But, as the Cory Report makes clear, 'However interpreted, the comment, if it was made, was clearly demeaning, if not threatening, to Rosemary Nelson.'

In June 1998, Rosemary Nelson sent a letter to the Investigating Officer at Castlereagh Holding Centre in Belfast in which she focused on derogatory remarks allegedly directed at her client (Client J), and added that 'this is part of an ongoing situation which quite frankly is unacceptable'. To quote the Cory Report, Client J's statement said that RUC officers had spoken to him about a man who had been shot in the head and 'that could be arranged to happen to him'. They also allegedly suggested he 'get a steel cage in his house for protection', that his details would be passed to the LVF and that he was being watched by the UDR 'who might also pass his details on to Loyalists'. They also allegedly 'referred to the murder of Robert Hamill in a way that suggested that he might meet a similar fate', and also about Rosemary Nelson allegedly saying that 'she is a Provo solicitor' and that she had got him 'well trained in anti-interrogation tactics'.

As mentioned in the previous chapter, there was an incident on the Garvaghy Road on 5 July 1997 while Rosemary Nelson was representing the GRRC, when she was allegedly assaulted by RUC officers as well as allegedly being verbally abused. The Cory Report refers to a note on a statement made by Rosemary Nelson from a member of the Committee on the Administration of Justice (CAJ) (a human rights organisation that works independently to promote better human rights for all parts of the political make-up of Northern Ireland) 'indicating that Rosemary Nelson's right arm was visibly bruised'. A Member of the Bar in the State of New York was also present, and gave a statement on 8 July 1997, which 'appeared to confirm Rosemary Nelson's account' of the incident.

Later, when the Colin Port inquiry team began gathering evidence in late March 1999, Rosemary's husband Paul confirmed that she had spoken to him about the threats. Mr Nelson said that he did not see the letter threats and thought they had been destroyed and that Rosemary 'did not like bringing them home', to quote the Cory Report. But Mr Nelson did tell an investigating officer to speak to a secretary in Rosemary's office. That secretary confirmed that there had been 'a number of threats' received. She mentioned a letter that Rosemary had received in November 1998, which she thought had been destroyed, but that threats became more prevalent during the Drumcree Conflict period with Rosemary's representation of the GRRC.

The secretary added that Rosemary did 'not appear to take the threats seriously, at least in the presence of office staff', and confirmed that a coded message had been received by another solicitor in the office while Rosemary was at court. This solicitor told investigators on 24 March 1999 that he had taken a call 'a day or two' before the Orange parade was scheduled to take place in Portadown. To quote the Cory Report, the man on the line said, 'This is the LVF. Tell Rosemary Nelson we will be at the march in Portadown and we will see what is going on.' Apparently, the caller then used words that the solicitor took to be code, either 'Blue Lagoon' or 'Blue Platoon'. The solicitor also thought that Rosemary might have sent copies of threatening letters to the CAJ, and this opinion was backed up by another employee. The solicitor employed in Rosemary's office also said that, just before Christmas 1998, Rosemary had told him that 'when she returned to her parked car four persons had driven up beside her, stopped, glared at her and then driven off'. Rosemary had also shown him 'a card or document' on which was written 'We know what you are'.

This male solicitor had also had a call put through to him after a receptionist took a call in the office. That receptionist told investigators on 24 March 1999 that the caller, a man with a local accent, had said, 'Just tell Rosemary this – the LVF and UVF will be joining with the Blue Platoons and they will be policing the Orange Parade in Portadown.'

On the same day, another employee was interviewed and spoke about the alleged threats made by the RUC to Rosemary's clients while held at Gough Barracks and the Castlereagh Holding Centre. The employee remembered a statement she had taken from a client who had reported he had been told, 'You're going to die when you get out and tell Rosemary she's going to die, too.' This employee in Rosemary Nelson's office also said about her employer, 'I think the ones from the police were the ones which scared her most.'

The Cory Report documents that Rosemary Nelson received a bullet in the post in 1997. Rosemary showed this bullet to three people – a friend, an official at BIRW and a member of the Irish Civil Service, the latter confirming that the bullet was meant for an automatic rifle. As the Cory Report states, 'There is no evidence that it came to the attention of either the RUC or any British governmental agency.'

As mentioned in the Prologue of this book, on 3 June

1998, Rosemary Nelson was the recipient of a handwritten note sent to her office which read: 'We have you in our sights, you republican bastard... we will teach you a lesson. RIP.' The Cory Report states that 'not surprisingly, this letter worried Rosemary Nelson', and she showed it to a number of people, including her husband, a BIRW official, the CAJ, a friend and a journalist. The direct nature of this threat, as the Cory Report states, 'became highly significant in connection with subsequent events'.

Also mentioned in the previous chapter, there was the pamphlet doing the rounds around Drumcree in July 1998. Titled *The Man Without a Future*, it alluded to the threat against a 'Mr M' (Brendan MacCionnaith, leader of the GRRC), who, the pamphlet alleged, 'became close friends with Mr N, now IRA Chief-of-Staff and his second-in-command, Mr O. These two men have been pulling Mr M's strings since he left gaol.' The pamphlet accused Mr M of trying to 'destroy the religious rights and freedoms of Hungarian Protestants by bringing them into conflict with the State', and went on to declare, 'Mr M, your plan has been found out, your time running out.' But the pamphlet also named Rosemary Nelson, gave her office address and phone number, linking her to Mr M by stating 'with advice from Lurgan solicitor and former bomber Rosemary Nelson'. This was an example of unfounded rumours and allegations about Rosemary Nelson being an active paramilitary member. The pamphlet ended with the highlighted warning: 'Ask not for whom the bell tolls... it tolls for you, Mr M.'

As the Cory Report tells us, 'an internal memorandum from the RUC, dated 7 August 1998, stated that the police had been informed by the NIO that Rosemary Nelson was extremely distressed by the leaflet and by the circulation of her office address and telephone number.' It was BIRW and the CAJ who passed the pamphlet on to the NIO, who, in turn, passed it on to Chief Constable of the RUC Sir Ronnie Flanagan 'on two occasions'.

The Cory Report on Rosemary Nelson also documents a threatening passage later found in the diary of ex-UVF commander and LVF founder Billy Wright. As Cory states, 'When Billy Wright's diary was made public, it was found to contain a passage that was clearly threatening to both Client A and his solicitor, Rosemary Nelson.' It should be remembered here that Billy Wright had encountered Rosemary Nelson, or at least knew of her presence at the Drumcree marches dispute, when she was representing the GRRC.

The main point to focus on here is why Rosemary Nelson was not warned of Wright's written threat to her. We know that she was a potential target for certain Loyalists through the other death threats made to her, but why was she not warned about this particular threat by a leading Loyalist, actually the head of a prominent breakaway paramilitary cell? As Cory reports, 'The documents from the Billy Wright file would seem to clearly indicate that the contents of the diary were not known to either Rosemary Nelson or the police prior to her murder.' It also states that Wright's personal effects in his cell (including his diary) were not taken by the RUC after his murder, but that they were handed out among other LVF prisoners in his wing. These were later collected and given to Wright's father, David Wright. The RUC only took possession of the clothes that Wright was wearing when he was murdered. The conclusion drawn is that the authorities did not know of the contents of Wright's diary until it was too late to warn Rosemary Nelson. As Cory reports, 'It could be argued that the RUC should have searched Billy Wright's cell and recovered the diary. However, it may be inferred that they considered it more important to search the cells of his murderers immediately after the killing.'

However, the fact that such a 'passage that was clearly threatening' was written down by Billy Wright in his personal diary shows the hatred and animosity felt towards Rosemary. As we shall see later, Wright was a charismatic leader who received great loyalty from his followers, and his opinion would have carried great sway with them. Therefore, the passage in Wright's diary can only be seen as an indirect threat against Rosemary Nelson, but is useful to show that she was indeed on the minds of Loyalists at senior levels.

A group of American lawyers visited Northern Ireland in February 1999 and had a meeting with the RUC Chief Constable Sir Ronnie Flanagan. On that trip, the American lawyers also met up with Rosemary Nelson, and she told them about her fears and the alleged threats told to her by clients, purportedly coming from RUC officers. She also told them about an incident that had happened in a local supermarket while she was shopping. It seems that she was being followed by 'a large man that she had not seen before', as Cory states. When she was alone with no other shoppers around, he approached her and said, 'If you don't stop representing IRA scum, you'll be dead.'

5

THE SILENCING

15 MARCH 1999
Lurgan, approximately 12.40pm

On the previous evening, which was Mother's Day, Rosemary Nelson had returned home from a weekend spent in the family's mobile-home getaway in Bundoran in Donegal. When she got in, she called her mother, Sheila Magee, to wish her a happy Mother's Day. Her mother later recalled the conversation, saying that Rosemary had spoken about the cold weather and the unusual helicopter presence in the vicinity of her home on Ashford Grange, to the west of the Kilwilkie Estate. It was the last time that Sheila spoke to her daughter, as Rosemary would never get to work the following day, although she got into her car to go there.

Rosemary's silver BMW (which had had a full service ten days earlier) was just approaching the junction close to her home. Opposite was Tannaghmore Primary School where her daughter was playing in the playground. When Rosemary braked at the junction, slowing her progress, the mercury tilt switch on the bomb attached underneath her car was triggered. That bomb contained 1lb of powergel explosives. To stop the bomb falling off of the car's underside, the bombers had also attached an industrial-strength magnet to the bomb, believed to be stolen from the Harland & Wolff shipyard in Belfast. In all, it was a sophisticated device. The explosion was deafening and was heard by Rosemary's daughter Sarah. The force of the blast tore apart the floor of the BMW.

But Rosemary was still conscious and speaking when people rushed to the scene. Her legs had been almost torn off, and her abdomen had been ripped apart. Rosemary's next-door neighbour was a nurse and was one of the first at the scene, trying to offer help. Rosemary's sister Bernie was at home having lunch and ran to the wrecked car as soon as she heard the explosion. As Rosemary's other sister Caitlin told the *Irish News* in 2003, 'Bernie was holding her hand and telling Rosemary to fight, telling her it was the biggest fight she would ever have.'

Calls were going out for an ambulance and a doctor. Within five minutes of the blast, a nurse arrived at the scene, and a doctor who had been contacted directly was on hand, and an ambulance then arrived. An RUC car then pulled up, according to a witness, allegedly 'very slowly... almost nonchalantly', and two RUC officers got out of the vehicle 'without any haste'. The Pat Finucane Centre later took witness statements after an appeal for information in Lurgan.

By 1.00pm, the RIR had the scene sealed off. Two RUC Land Rovers then arrived (which had both been seen earlier). By now, the riot squad was also present, there was a helicopter hovering overhead, and the Army had blocked off the end of the nearby North Circular Road. A crowd made up of local residents was growing, and there were also two army Land Rovers spotted on Lake Street near by.

At 1.10pm, a fire engine arrived on the scene and Rosemary was rushed to hospital and into the operating theatre. Tragically, there was little that the doctors could do to save her and Rosemary Nelson died around two hours after the explosion.

Confirmation of Rosemary's death reached the bomb scene at 3.10pm.

Less than an hour after Rosemary's death was announced, local residents of the Kilwilkie Estate, mainly Nationalists, marched to the centre of Lurgan and held a vigil of a minute's silence outside Rosemary's office in William Street.

Rosemary Nelson was 40 years old and left behind a husband and three children aged 8, 11 and 13, the youngest of whom, Sarah, had heard the explosion that ripped through her mother's body and shattered their lives. It was two days before St Patrick's Day, a day of joy and celebration.

Rosemary's sister Bernie had spoken to her the night before her murder, and Rosemary had mentioned that there was a great deal of helicopter activity close to her home. Other witnesses would also come forward to say that there had been a much higher security presence in the area than usual in the days, weeks and even months before the bomb was planted and exploded.

It is important to remember that Lurgan at this time, less than a year after the signing of the Good Friday Agreement and the so-called end of the Troubles, always had a security force presence. But the information reported below indicates extraordinary security activity that struck local people, including Rosemary herself on the evening before her death, as far more active than usual. The critical question is – what was the reason for the increased security presence. But this in turn poses the question: how did the bombers gain access to Rosemary Nelson's car to plant the bomb, especially, as we shall see, two visits were required to achieve this successfully?

The increased security activity witnessed by local people and collated by the Pat Finucane Centre in the area of North Lurgan actually began up to three months before 15 March, at the start of 1999. From this time, there were more RUC and RIR Land Rover and foot patrols in the area. Added to this, there were also many checkpoints set up. There was marked activity in the fields close to Tannaghmore Primary School, a very short distance from Rosemary Nelson's home and where her daughter attended. Patrols were also witnessed being set down by helicopter in February and March and, by mid- to late February, searchlights were seen scanning the fields close to Rosemary's home.

At about this time, an RUC and RIR presence was noted in the area, including one RUC and four army vehicles, with about six people standing and more in the vehicles. Among these, two ordinary cars were noted, and a witness stated that it looked like 'the RUC and Army were giving cover to the men with the civilian cars'. Helicopter landings were occurring frequently now, with some hovering above, and one was noted landing in the field of a local man close to Tannaghmore Primary School, a witness saying that 'this hasn't happened before'. A week later, there was 'unusual' security activity in the vicinity of nearby Mile House and vehicle checkpoints were mobilised at around midday, as well as an earlier one on Shore Road. Soldiers were also seen being dropped off close to Rosemary Nelson's house at the beginning of March. A witness stated that Rosemary, in her office, had made comments about the RUC and RIR security activity around her house at this time.

A week before Rosemary's murder, RUC and RIR personnel were spotted going into a field in the Mile House area. Between eight and ten soldiers were noted there. On 9 March, just six days before the bomb exploded, a helicopter was seen landing multiple times around midday, with very short lengths of time between landings, making a witness feel that soldiers must have been collected from a nearby army base in Portadown. Three days after that, there was an RUC checkpoint in operation at the junction of Victoria Street, and two army Land Rovers were seen on an industrial estate driving towards Mile House.

That takes us to the weekend before Rosemary's murder – 13 and 14 March. That Saturday, a strong security presence was witnessed in the area, with a witness overhearing an English accent. By lunchtime, there were RUC and RIR patrols and vehicle checkpoints in place. Three army Land Rovers were also seen in a car park close to Rosemary's office on William Street, Lurgan. One of the reasons that local witnesses remembered the activity, especially the presence of the RIR, was that there was no discernible trouble in the area. The Army was usually sent out in response to an incident at this time, but there was none. It looked as if some kind of preparations were being made for something. There was also helicopter activity that day, with a chopper hovering over the nearby Kilwilkie Estate for a prolonged period between 6.00pm and midnight. Various witness accounts state that helicopters had a red or green light on at night.

On Sunday, 14 March, the day before the murder, the helicopter presence continued, and was occurring at the time that local people went to Mass at 10.45am. An hour later, a helicopter was seen hovering again, sometimes coming down surprisingly low to the ground. By this time, there was also a checkpoint on Edward Street, operated by the RIR and only checking vehicles leaving Lurgan. 'Heavy' RUC and RIR security activity was once again seen around about Tannaghmore Primary School, very close to Rosemary's house and to where the bomb would explode. In the field at the bottom of Rosemary's street, there was also much security movement seen. A witness would also say that they could not sleep that afternoon because of the helicopter noise. This helicopter activity would continue in the Shore Road area until 10.00pm that night. Such activity was only more noticeable as it was a Sunday. One witness reported that helicopter action continued until around 2.30am.

One helicopter seen that day flying very low above the fields behind Tannaghmore Primary School at around 5.00pm drew particular attention. It was a Lynx, and this was unusual, as a Gazelle was the usual helicopter seen in the area. It also had a 'heli-tele', a broadcast-standard television surveillance system, attached to it. Both helicopters and Land Rovers were seen in the area for the rest of the evening, and choppers were still seen 'a way after midnight' according to a witness, another saying that one of them was hovering so low as if it might 'land on the house'. One witness told the Pat Finucane Centre that they saw a helicopter at around 7.30pm that evening 'tilting… moving backwards and forwards', and that it 'seemed to be looking for something on the ground'. It was also thought strange that the Land Rovers were present, as there was no discernible checkpoint (although they were seen at around 11.30pm on Church Place), and spotlights were seen coming from RUC Land Rovers. There were also children seen throwing stones in the area, but this was hardly reason enough for the high-security presence and search actions.

At 10.30pm, two witnesses saw a helicopter very close to Tannaghmore Primary School. Both said that a green light was emanating from it, one saying, 'if it were not for the sound of the helicopter, I would have mistaken it for a star'. The last reported sighting of a helicopter that night was at 2.30am on the morning of Monday, 15 March. A helicopter hum was next heard at around 6.00am by a mother up feeding her baby. Ninety minutes later, a line of RUC Land Rovers were spotted going into Lurgan RUC station, and, half-an-hour later, an RIR patrol was seen on Shore Road, and an RUC Land Rover at a house for around 20 minutes. Between 9.05am and 9.20am, two RIR and one RUC Land Rover were seen in the area and at 10.00am there was an RIR foot patrol witnessed on Lake Street at the railway junction.

A witness also saw two RIR soldiers at 10.00am, the first putting something in the other's rucksack. Other witnesses in a taxi saw an RIR and RUC foot patrol of around seven or eight men at the railway tracks. One was seen picking up something from behind the railway control box which looked like an 'aerosol can with wires attached', and the soldier told a civilian witness that it was a suspect device. The witness considered this strange, as the area was not sealed off as it usually would be in such a situation. Also at 10.00am, an RIR soldier was seen taking an 'object' of about seven or eight inches long out of a hedge and putting it in another soldier's rucksack.

Five minutes later, RUC officers were seen wearing boiler suits in the car park inside the Lurgan RUC station, as well as a red 'dog van' with a handler. One of the officers was also later seen at Rosemary's bombed-out car. Land Rovers continued to be spotted for the rest of the morning. Between 11.15am and 11.20am, three civilians were walking down the Old Portadown Road when two RUC Land Rovers pulled over. Four officers in boiler suits got out of the first and blocked the onward path of the civilians, two of whom stopped, and the one who did not later said that he was 'p-checked' (number plate check) and subjected to a full body search. He added that one of the RUC officers 'verbally abused' one of his friends. As the three walked away, the witness reported that officers shouted abuse at them.

At around 12.40pm, Rosemary Nelson's BMW exploded at the junction next to Tannaghmore Primary School.

The Chief Constable of the RUC, Sir Ronnie Flanagan, drafted in the help of John Guido of the FBI and the Chief Constable of Kent David Phillips to direct the investigation into Rosemary Nelson's murder, although their involvement would prove to be a supervisory one rather than 'on the ground'. Such a high-profile approach was necessary for there to be any credibility in the RUC's investigation among the Catholic community and internationally. Rosemary Nelson had become an international figure in legal/political circles and her testimony before the US Congress had made her a very significant figure in the United States. And the involvement of the FBI was not an unprecedented move, as they had assisted in investigations in Northern Ireland before. The lack of faith in the RUC (whether founded or unfounded) among the Catholic community should also not be underestimated. To make a thorough and proper investigation, the RUC would have had to get the co-operation of many in the Lurgan Catholic community, the very section of the population that was highly suspicious of the RUC. Knowledge of the alleged threats and abuses purportedly given out to Rosemary Nelson by RUC officers deepened this suspicion and therefore resistance to any co-operation with them strengthened. Likewise, allegations about rumoured collusion over a decade, in the murders of Patrick Finucane in 1989, Sam Marshall in 1990 and Robert Hamill in 1997, were firmly in the minds of many. To use an Irish expression, 'The dogs in the street knew.'

One of the first prominent statements made in the wake of Rosemary Nelson's assassination (it can be called that as the motives for killing her had a political element) was from Bertie Ahern, the Taoiseach of the Republic of Ireland. He said that it had sent 'shockwaves through the international community' and that it was the 'assassination of one of the leading people in the world of law'. Then President Bill Clinton, who, of course, had had a hand in the forging of the Good Friday Agreement in the previous year, said that it was 'a despicable and cowardly act by the enemies of peace'. New Jersey Congressman Chris Smith said that it was 'a gross atrocity' and that the British Government led by Tony Blair had to 'follow every lead, even if it implicates security forces and the police'. This latter remark was direct and to the point, and was an early indication of the international level of suspicion over alleged State collusion.

Within hours of Rosemary Nelson's murder, another statement was made. But this time it was a coded one sent to the BBC, claiming responsibility for her killing. The group claiming responsibility was called the Red Hand Defenders, a Loyalist splinter group, which had been declared illegal just weeks before Rosemary's murder. However, those who knew the sectarian reality on the streets had no doubt that this organisation was a front for the LVF and perhaps the Orange Volunteers.

After the murder of former UVF unit commander and LVF founder 'King Rat' Billy Wright inside the Maze Prison on 27 December 1997, the command of the LVF passed to Mark Fulton, known as 'Swinger'. With Wright gone, and his hatred of Rosemary Nelson recorded in his diary – the gist of which was that Rosemary might be a lawyer, but that did not offer her any protection – his successor undoubtedly felt the same way about Rosemary. Enter Mark 'Swinger' Fulton, leader of the LVF, into Rosemary Nelson's story.

Mark Fulton was born on a working-class estate in Portadown, in the area called Killycomain in 1961. His mother came from a family of wealthy car dealers, but, according to a *Sunday Tribune* article of 16 June 2002, she 'married beneath her', choosing Jim Fulton, known as 'Old Swinger', as her husband. Fulton Sr was a former British soldier and then made his living as a window cleaner. However, as the Troubles deepened in the early 1970s, Jim Fulton became increasingly involved with the UDA and Loyalist paramilitary activity and, according to the *Sunday Tribune*, the house in which little Mark grew up was a meeting place for prominent Loyalists of the period. One childhood friend remembered the young Mark as being a 'lovely, sweet wee boy'. This was very different to the reputation that Fulton gained as a man. A neighbour from Fulton's childhood helped to explain how this transformation took place: 'When you are fed poison, is it any wonder it enters your bloodstream?'

Susan Mackay of the *Sunday Tribune* explored this further in her 2002 article: 'Young Swinger followed the traditional route into Loyalist paramilitarism – leaving school early, induction into criminality, followed by blooding in sectarian murder.' Just as in the Mafia it was alleged that a potential member had to make a kill to become a 'made' man, the same kind of induction seems to have been required to become a fully trusted member of some extreme paramilitary groups. When Mark Fulton returned from school, his home was an environment in which sectarian talk was rife.

The strength of Mark Fulton's feelings of bitterness about the abuse of Protestants in Northern Ireland over the centuries can be gauged from his writings in the sporadic LVF 'magazine' *Leading the Way*, which was sold outside Drumcree Church during the conflict there. In a 1998 edition, which was a tribute to the recently murdered Billy Wright, and when Swinger was leader of the LVF, he laid out his feelings in this historical context.

Fulton went back as far as 1641 and the period of the Planters, writing how pregnant Protestant women 'had their foetuses cut from their wombs and fed to dogs' and about the drowning of thousands of Protestants in the River Bann.

Fulton was also very concerned and angry about the dissolution of the Protestant Irish tradition and culture over the years. In another piece he wrote, his target was the Alliance Party, which was supporting 'integrated' education, a policy he wrote was 'designed to rob all our young people of all knowledge of their culture'. This weakening of his culture enraged him so much that he also wrote that if you were in the vicinity of Alliance headquarters and 'just happened to have a petrol bomb with you...' Nothing more needed to be said, and there was such an attack later. This ingrained philosophy of fear and hate sounds more like Apartheid-era South Africa than Northern Ireland in the late 1990s, but this illustrates how close political/religious sectarianism comes to racism, as Rosemary Nelson pointed out shortly before her murder.

Fulton's politics, like his mentor Billy Wright's, were motivated by similar grievances to the mainstream Democratic Unionist Party (DUP), led by Ian Paisley, who was actually one of the first to come out against Rosemary Nelson's murder in a statement. As already mentioned, Billy Wright was hugely charismatic and his life-and-death passion for his cause was very influential on his unit in the UVF and later the LVF. His effect on his deputy in the LVF, and later his successor, Mark Fulton was absolute, so much so that the *Sunday Tribune* termed them 'blood brothers'. An interviewee told that newspaper in 2002 that they were 'unusually close'.

This was undoubtedly true. In fact, Mark Fulton had a tattoo of Billy Wright over his heart, inked on after Wright's murder. This symbol of loyalty to his mentor and the cause they fought for could hardly have been more eloquent as to Fulton's sympathies. Also, Fulton was known to have spent nights alone at Wright's grave in private vigil. Fulton would have died for Wright, and Wright had known that only too well. Whether this loyalty would have been reciprocated is not fully known, and Wright had immense control over Fulton, a man infamous for his incendiary temper. A former associate of them both said in 2002, 'Swinger had a temper. Billy was the only one [who] could control him.' A detective who had professional dealings with these two dangerous men said that Wright was 'coolness personified', while Fulton was very vocal and threatening; he was, in effect, Wright's 'rottweiler' and protector. Fulton idolised Wright and would have gone to the ends of the earth for him. While Wright was clinical in his violence, Fulton was more impulsive and trigger-happy. As a former associate of Fulton told the *Sunday Tribune* in 2002, Fulton was 'a sprayer, not a sayer', referencing his reputation for firing bullets.

Billy Wright lived in a large detached house on the fringe of Brownstown in Portadown. Fulton, a heavy drinker who had a wife and two children, lived on the Hobson Park council estate to the rear of Wright. They were two of the most notorious Loyalists of their generation, and their strong bond and differing personalities added colour to their legend.

In the early 1990s, when Wright and Fulton were in the UVF and known as 'the Rat Pack', it is thought that

Fulton was involved in at least 12 murders, the victims being largely Catholic, who faced an inquisition about their religion before they were shot. Unlike the Shankill Butchers, who were notorious for hideous physical torture before the dispatch of their victims, the torture here was usually mental, although some were diabolically shot in front of their families. In this period, Fulton was pulled in on suspicion of murder, but never convicted of it, although he was for extortion.

Before his murder in the Maze Prison on 27 December 1997, Billy Wright had formulated a plan to murder Catholics, according to the *Sunday Tribune*, in partnership with the UDA. After Wright's murder, Fulton put this plan into action, and Rosemary Nelson was murdered 15 months after Billy Wright was killed. It was also three weeks after the inquest into Wright's death had been concluded. As a source told the *Daily Herald* in 2002, 'A number of paramilitaries had attended the inquest. It's certainly likely that they were emotionally stirred up and decided to kill Rosemary by way of some backhanded send off to their hero.' As we retrospectively know from Wright's diary, he had already singled her out. The murder of Rosemary Nelson was very possibly a trigger effect of revenge for Wright's murder, mixed with the plan for the murders of Catholics already laid down by the deceased LVF leader.

As we know, the INLA prisoners killed Wright because he was continuing to run the LVF from his Maze cell, as they said in their statement claiming responsibility for his murder. Fulton was so close to Wright and his anguish over his mentor's violent death cut so deep that the effect of Wright's death on the targeting of Catholics and the murder of Rosemary Nelson in particular cannot be underestimated. Fulton wrote of Wright's nobility and conviction in the *Leading the Way* tribute issue, saying about his hero that he 'knew his job was to protect the civil rights and culture of his people'. Fulton felt his responsibility to his people just as Wright had. But, of course, it shouldn't be forgotten that, like Billy Wright, Fulton was known to be a drug-dealer, as the *Daily Herald* reminded us in 2002.

After Wright's death, the LVF under Fulton's leadership often used the front name of the 'Red Hand Defenders' when claiming responsibility for their actions. The possible make-up of Rosemary Nelson's bombing team will be discussed later, but there is no doubt that Mark Fulton was the mastermind behind her killing, and this fact entered the public domain in 2002. But, when the device under Rosemary's BMW exploded just after midday on Monday, 15 March 1999, Mark Fulton was actually in prison.

Fulton had been arrested in 1998 when he fired shots at an off-duty soldier in the street. Fulton was drunk at the time. He was convicted of this attack, and sentenced to four years, being held in Maghaberry Prison in County Antrim. But just as Wright had done inside the Maze, Fulton continued to direct LVF operations from inside the jail, increasingly using the 'Red Hand Defenders' moniker for attacks.

The ruthlessness of Fulton and the LVF at this time should not be underestimated. In 1998, punishment was meted out to an LVF member suspected of being an informer. David Keys, a fellow prisoner in the jail, was slashed, badly beaten and anally raped with a snooker cue and then strangled to death. Those who crossed Fulton and the LVF could be in no doubt of the consequences. However, this very ruthlessness would later be turned on Fulton himself as his power within the LVF and Loyalist circles began to slip.

Just before Rosemary Nelson's murder, Mark Fulton had been released from prison for a short spell on compassionate leave. This is when he is believed to have given the final instructions for her assassination. He was also seen on the day of her murder waiting anxiously next to a radio in prison, obviously expecting news of her murder. The long-standing death threats against Rosemary Nelson had finally been carried out. Fulton's LVF, in revenge for their leader Billy Wright's murder by the rival Republican paramilitary unit, the INLA, and as part of a plan to murder Catholics set down by Wright, had made sure it happened.

The day following Rosemary Nelson's murder saw a huge outpouring of official statements from powerful people of all political persuasions. The British Prime Minister Tony Blair stated that it was a 'disgusting act of barbarity' and that every effort would be made in 'hunting down' those who were involved in her murder. Blair was also concerned that such a high-profile assassination could derail the still fragile peace process, still in its early days. This was echoed by the Minister of Foreign Affairs David Andrews who said that those responsible had to be caught and quickly. Paul Murphy, the Minister for Political Development in Northern Ireland, stated that 'while it is too early to speculate on who was responsible for this horrific incident, we will leave no stone unturned in the effort to bring the perpetrators of this evil crime to justice'. In London, the high-profile charismatic Labour MP Ken Livingstone said that he was going to table an Early Day Motion in the House of Commons demanding that the Government look into the security arrangements taken to protect Rosemary before her murder.

The President of Sinn Fein, Gerry Adams, expressed his shock and said that 'the attack on Rosemary Nelson is an attack on the Good Friday Agreement which proclaims the right of citizens to live free from sectarian abuse'. A friend of Rosemary Nelson, Sinn Fein Assembly member Dara O'Hagan, stated that 'this was an attack carried out by experienced people and was not the work of amateur Loyalist groups'. Mary Robinson, the UN High Commissioner for Human Rights, said that 'her death has sad echoes of the murder of Pat Finucane and comes at a particularly sensitive time in the peace process'.

Seamus Mallon, then a member of the Northern Ireland Assembly and soon to be the first Deputy First Minister of Northern Ireland, said that the murder 'shows in a murderous and grotesque way how important the peace process is and that nothing must be allowed to endanger the cause of peace'. The leader of the Ulster Unionist Party David Trimble, who represented the constituency in which Lurgan is located, expressed his horror and sent his sympathy to the Nelson family. Trimble's deputy, John Taylor, showed his condemnation of Rosemary's murder 'without reservation' on behalf of his party and added that 'whilst Unionists would have disagreed with Rosemary Nelson's views and actions, murder can never be condoned'. The veteran leader of the DUP, Ian Paisley, said, 'A mother is dead and her children have been left without a mother.'

The SDLP Assembly member Brid Rodgers, meanwhile, lauded Rosemary Nelson for her support of the family of Robert Hamill and of the GRRC, saying that 'she defended the basic human rights of a vulnerable and exposed community'. Another personal tribute came from the Women's Coalition, who said that it was the responsibility of people to make sure that her murder made stronger 'the principles of justice, by which she lived'. Catherine Dixon, the President of the Northern Ireland Law Society, said that Rosemary's murder was an obvious act to frighten the legal profession and that 'solicitors have worked over many years of the Troubles to provide the best possible service to the entire community', a principle that was embodied in Rosemary Nelson's decision throughout her career to represent both sides of the political divide. Protests and gatherings to remember Rosemary occurred all over Northern Ireland and in London.

The Chairman of the Police Authority, Pat Armstrong, gave his full support to RUC Chief Constable Sir Ronnie Flanagan. Supporting the calling in of outside help in the investigation of Rosemary's murder, Armstrong said, 'We would applaud the Chief Constable's speedy action in this matter and would give our full support to his decision.' However, the brother of the murdered defence lawyer Pat Finucane, Martin Finucane, said that Flanagan's calling in of David Phillips, the Chief Constable of Kent, to the investigation was 'pathetic and inept' and that only an independent international inquiry would suffice.

David Phillips, Chief Constable of Kent, arrived in

Northern Ireland the next day to start overseeing the investigation into Rosemary's murder, and the RUC was already conferring with the FBI. The Sinn Fein President Gerry Adams responded by saying, 'clearly this mechanism of appointing English policemen to get at the truth will find no support or confidence among Nationalists'. This view would continue to be amplified among Republicans, and would cloud the investigation as it progressed. Brid Rodgers, the member of the Northern Ireland Assembly for Upper Bann and soon to be Minister for Agriculture and Rural Development, echoed this mindset. She said, 'I am concerned about the independence of the investigation... I think the primary investigators should be an outside police force and that the role of the RUC in this should be very much secondary.' The Chief Commissioner of the Northern Ireland Human Rights Commission, Brice Dickson, also added, 'The Human Rights Commission believes that allegations of collusion between the RUC and paramilitaries can be effectively and credibly investigated only by officers from outside the RUC.' This statement by a neutral organisation added to the disquiet about an English Chief Constable leading the investigation.

There was also a protest outside the Lurgan RUC station, and the GRRC spokesman and friend of Rosemary Nelson, Breandan Mac Cionnaith, accused Tony Blair of being negligent in failing to protect Rosemary. As we know, requests had been made for her protection through Jonathan Powell, Blair's Chief of Staff, but Mac Cionnaith told the crowd that they had been ignored. The NIO swiftly released a statement saying that 'third-party approaches' had been made on

Rosemary's behalf to the British Government, but that Rosemary had never approached them personally herself.

That same day, 17 March, two days after Rosemary Nelson's murder, another murder took place on the Shankill Road in Belfast. A strongly Loyalist area, the killing was of a Loyalist and shows the internecine political wrangling within the Loyalist cause.

The man's body was found to the rear of the Pony Trotting Sports & Social Club. He had been shot in the back of the head several times. He was Frankie Curry, aged 46, and was an ex-member of the dissident group the Red Hand Commando, a Loyalist unit with strong links to the UVF. This group had spawned a further splinter group – the Red Hand Defenders – the group that had claimed responsibility for Rosemary Nelson's murder, and was actually the LVF in all but name.

As we have seen, Billy Wright, who founded the LVF after breaking away from the UVF after growing disillusioned with their direction, was very divisive within Loyalist circles. Anybody who sided with Billy Wright and his cause of zero co-operation with the peace process, before and after Wright's murder in December 1997 (the LVF torch passing to Mark Fulton), was now an enemy of the UVF and its leaders. Frankie Curry was just such a victim of his loyalty to Wright. Curry had been thrown out of the Red Hand Commando for 'treason', the worst possible charge in paramilitary circles. Curry had recently moved to Portadown, the area where Billy Wright had been most powerful.

The RUC swiftly stated that it believed three gunmen had carried out Curry's murder, and passers-by saw a man running fast down the Shankill Road around the time of the shooting. The area was sealed off for forensic tests and the RUC tried to trace a man believed to have been with Curry when he was attacked.

The mother of Frankie Curry was rushed to hospital when she collapsed on hearing of her son's murder.

That very evening, just 48 hours after they had announced that they had executed Rosemary Nelson, the Red Hand Defenders issued another statement. It read: 'We knew that Frank Curry was murdered by the UVF today.' This again reinforces just how splintered the Loyalists had become during the burgeoning peace process and the recent signing of the Good Friday Agreement.

The Red Hand Defenders also made threats of military action against named UVF leaders, and even towards the PUP, the political wing of the UVF.

Sinn Fein President Gerry Adams spoke from Washington, DC, asking for calm and saying, 'People have to make sure that the wreckers do not get their way.' Also in Washington, the then Northern Ireland Secretary Dr Mo Mowlam said, 'This was an appalling killing as was the death of Rosemary Nelson. Killings like this serve no purpose.'

Spokesman for the Ulster Democratic Party (UDP) John White also agreed that Loyalists had gunned down Curry. White said, 'It is disgraceful that a man who dedicated his life to the Loyalist cause should be cut down like this by people who call themselves Loyalists.' However, as with most violence in sectarian circles in Northern Ireland, a murky shadow had followed Frankie Curry in life, and the *Irish News* dubbed him a 'notorious paramilitary'. Indeed, just before his murder,

Curry had boasted to journalists that he had carried out a 'series of killings'. This domino effect of violence is one that is all too familiar.

Eight months before Rosemary Nelson and Frankie Curry were murdered, it is believed almost certainly that Curry murdered a man because of a personal grudge. In July 1998, 49-year-old Paul Wassy was shot dead outside his home in Bangor, County Down, as he came back from the newsagent with the morning papers. Wassy's widow Sarah reported seeing the assassin, who was wearing a red, white and blue balaclava, get into a Ford Orion car (later reportedly driven by another Loyalist). Sarah was sure that the masked gunman was Frankie Curry, as she recognised his 'distinctive, sloping run', as she said at her husband's inquest.

Paul Wassy and Frankie Curry did indeed have history. Their paths first crossed when Curry began intimidating Wassy's brother to get him to drop charges relating to another incident. Curry drove a car at Wassy's brother and then 'wounded him in a shooting', the inquest heard. In revenge for the attack on his brother, Paul Wassy followed Curry through Bangor. Sarah Wassy told the inquest, 'Wassy trailed Frankie Curry around and headbutted him. I heard Wassy tell him if he ever went near his family again he would beat him to death. He wouldn't need a gun.'

After this incident, Paul Wassy received several death threats, and this stirred him to approach members of Loyalist paramilitaries, who reassured him that their groups were not behind the threats; it was personal. To increase his personal security and that of his family, Wassy had CCTV cameras installed at his home. But this didn't prevent his murder. The inquest heard how Curry jumped from the boot of the Ford Orion and opened fire on Wassy. His widow Sarah then saw him lying in the square, his newspapers strewn next to him. Sarah told the inquest, 'Everything went into slow motion and I started screaming, "Frankie Curry shot my husband!"' It was later proven that the driver of the Ford Orion was a man called Thomas Maginnis, aged 44, who apparently had an IQ of 67.

No direct link was ever found between Frankie Curry and the murder of Rosemary Nelson. But his murder just two days after her own, and by his own side (though mortally fractured) shows just how ruthless and complex sectarian divisions and sub-divisions had become in Loyalist paramilitaries at the time of her murder, which was now causing international ripples. On the evening of Frankie Curry's murder, a vigil was held by candlelight outside the British Consulate in New York in protest at Rosemary's assassination.

On Thursday, 18 March, three days after her death, Rosemary Nelson's funeral took place at St Peter's Church. Thousands of mourners lined the streets and trailed the cortège as it wended its way from Rosemary's house to the church. It was a moving send-off for a woman who was popular and loved in her own community, but whose death had touched people far beyond her own hometown.

Immediately after the funeral, the leading British human rights lawyer Michael Mansfield QC called for an independent investigation followed by a judicial inquiry into Rosemary's murder.

6

THE COLLUSION QUESTION

On 19 March 1999, the day after Rosemary Nelson's funeral, the Ulster Unionist Party (UUP) leader David Trimble made some comments in interviews from Washington, DC, where he had been taking part in St Patrick's Day celebrations. Trimble had received the Nobel Peace Prize the previous year for his work towards peace in Northern Ireland and so his thoughts carried great weight internationally. He said that it was possible that the bomb attached to the underside of Rosemary's BMW was not placed there by Loyalists, but by Republicans. His reasoning for this was that the significant political and sectarian repercussions of Rosemary's murder played nicely into the hands of Republicans, and so enhanced their cause. Such comments show that, in the minds of some on the Loyalist side, there was doubt that one of their number had carried out the murder, at least publicly, despite the Red Hand Defenders taking immediate responsibility for it.

Such political views would inevitably be aired in the melting pot of tensions in Northern Ireland. But the biggest question being asked on the streets was whether there was any possibility of alleged State collusion in the murder. This question had already been raised in the cases of the murders of Sam Marshall and Robert Hamill by Rosemary Nelson herself, as well as the allegation that certain of her clients had reported that individual officers within the RUC had made death threats against her.

'Collusion' literally means co-operation or to jointly take part in something in a secretive way. The murder of soldiers and police officers in Northern Ireland during and since the Troubles is atrocious enough, the killing of civilians even more so. But the concern over question of State negligence, if not involvement, in certain cases of terrorism was ingrained among some observers and commentators in Northern Ireland as far back as the 1970s. Lawyers such as Pat Finucane and Rosemary Nelson, both murdered, raised the possibility of this in the 1980s and 1990s, the latter bringing it on to the international stage. Of course, the murder of Finucane ten years before Rosemary Nelson, and the parallels between the two cases, has also been subject to debate over the question of collusion.

The presence of bomb-makers and gunmen, getaway drivers and lookouts in Northern Ireland had long been par for the course. However, the allegation that the British Government could be negligent in allegedly turning a blind eye to certain atrocities, even if not complicit when it was politically convenient, is much more shocking. It also needs to be remembered that these allegations fall on both sides of the sectarian divide – for example, the questions about the murder of Loyalist leader Billy Wright discussed earlier should not be forgotten. The British Army, the RUC and the Northern Ireland Prison Service were, of course, the tools of the government for keeping order on the ground during times when Northern Ireland sometimes resembled the Wild West. If this allegation were true and one or other of these organisations had ever acted in a way that was not conducive to justice in the most basic and moral sense of the word, the entire rules of the game change. But this question of alleged State collusion continues to gnaw away at those seeking justice in Northern Ireland.

Ironically, the results of the investigation into the allegation that certain of Rosemary's clients reported that individual officers within the RUC had made death threats against her were due to be released that day also, four days after her murder. The results were not made public that day, but it soon became known that it was the ICPC who had forced the hand of the RUC Chief Constable Sir Ronnie Flanagan to remove the RUC from the investigation into the question of alleged death threats to Rosemary Nelson. The ICPC had approached Mo Mowlam directly, the first time it had done so on a case. A Metropolitan Police team took over. Flanagan made a press statement on 19 March thanking the FBI and the Kent Constabulary for their help on the Rosemary Nelson murder inquiry, adding that they would 'demonstrate honesty of purpose, professionalism and integrity in this investigation'.

In that same statement, Flanagan said that Sir John Stevens, then Deputy Commissioner of the Metropolitan Police, had been appointed to him to look into the murder of Pat Finucane ten years earlier. This had been prompted by a report by British Human Rights Watch, which had also been brought to the attention of Mo Mowlam. However, some people, including the Pat Finucane Centre, were less than happy about Stevens' involvement. A spokesman for the Pat Finucane Centre said that, due to Stevens' 'unsatisfactory' previous track record in reaching an outcome in investigating alleged collusion, Stevens should be 'the last person' to be appointed to the role. Mirroring the comments by Michael Mansfield QC the previous day for an independent judicial inquiry into Rosemary Nelson's murder, Amnesty International weighed in with a call to the British Government to institute such an inquiry to investigate allegations that the security forces had 'harassed' defence solicitors in Northern Ireland.

This charge of alleged harassment by State security forces had, of course, been raised by Rosemary Nelson several times, including in her address to the US Congress in Washington, DC. While vigils continued to be held for Rosemary, the ICPC spoke on her behalf. It said that in 1998 there had been 36 complaints lodged with them by 15 different Northern Ireland defence solicitors, including Rosemary. But, as Pat Finucane's former law partner Peter Madden said, this figure was very unrepresentative, as many lawyers had not lodged their complaints with the ICPC, but with British Human Rights Watch.

Also, it soon became clear that, while the FBI and the Kent Constabulary were overseeing the investigation into Nelson's murder, the RUC was conducting it on the ground. In a press statement, the Chief Constable of

Kent, David Phillips, and John Guido of the FBI said that they would 'provide independent and professional scrutiny' of the RUC investigation, but that the RUC was best placed to carry out the enormous groundwork required. It is true that the RUC knew its patch, but could it really be completely trusted with running an investigation into the murder of a woman who had made allegations of harassment against the RUC itself?

Two prominent politicians chimed in on this. SDLP Assembly member Brid Rodgers said, 'The SDLP is appalled by this declaration in the appropriateness of the RUC investigating the murder of Rosemary Nelson. One has to ask how such a statement could be made on the same day as the ICPC reports on the fact that it doubted the RUC's handling of Rosemary Nelson's allegations of police harassment to the extent that it referred the claims to the Metropolitan Police.'

Bairbre de Brun of Sinn Fein said, 'The ICPC adjudged the RUC incapable of investigating threats against Rosemary Nelson's life. How can Mr Phillips (of the Kent Constabulary) judge them capable of investigating her murder?'

However, Pat Armstrong, Chairman of the Northern Ireland Police Authority, disagreed, saying, 'It is hard to escape the conclusion that some of the recent commentators are not interested in securing the detection of Mrs Nelson's murderers, but are using her murder as a platform from which to attack the RUC.'

On 21 March, *Ireland on Sunday* reported that witnesses with potential evidence for the Nelson murder investigation would not co-operate with the RUC. The article focused on two witnesses who said that they would give their evidence to an independent inquiry, but not to the RUC. This would lead to members of the Pat Finucane Centre staff being asked to go to Lurgan three days later to gather evidence. As several newspapers began to speculate about dissident Loyalist involvement in Rosemary's murder, unrest broke out in Lurgan throughout that weekend. This prompted Sinn Fein to call for calm on 22 March, and Sinn Fein Assembly member Dara O'Hagan to make a demand for the withdrawal of the 'provocative' RUC from the Kilwilkie Estate, close to the Nelson home and to where she was killed. *Irish News* reported that the SDLP was going to challenge the fact that no member of the RUC had been suspended from duty in relation to the alleged threats against Rosemary Nelson.

The SDLP did just that. Brid Rodgers challenged then British Prime Minister Tony Blair to show his agreement with Bertie Ahern, Taoiseach of the Republic of Ireland, in calling for the investigation into Rosemary Nelson's murder to comprise independent investigators and that the RUC should be removed from an active role in it. There was no official response from Blair and, in fact, on 24 March the NIO Minister Lord Dubs said that the RUC would not be removed from the investigation, and that the RUC was most equipped to carry it out. Rodgers also said that Param Cumaraswamy, the UN Special Rapporteur who had investigated alleged threats and intimidation against Rosemary for the United Nations, should be part of the investigation.

The ICPC gave the Nelson family a copy of its full report into the question of alleged death threats to Rosemary Nelson, highlighting its 16 'serious concerns' about the RUC investigation into those alleged death threats before Rosemary's murder. To quote the Pat Finucane Centre, these included claims that RUC officers were 'hostile, evasive, disinterested and unco-operative and that a senior RUC officer made judgements about Rosemary Nelson's character and cast doubt on her professional integrity'. Another claim focused on 'the ill-disguised hostility to Mrs Nelson on the part of some police officers'.

This moved Rosemary's widower Paul Nelson to make a statement: 'If the ICPC had no confidence in the ability of the RUC to investigate the death threats against Rosemary, how can my family be expected to have confidence in their ability or indeed their willingness to effectively investigate her murder?'

That same day, Bertie Ahern repeated his call for the Nelson murder inquiry to be 'independent and transparent', and that David Phillips, Chief Constable of the Kent Constabulary, should have complete control of the investigation. On the other hand, the prominent Ulster Unionist Michael McGimpsey strongly denied that the RUC could have colluded with the Red Hand Defenders, who carried out Rosemary's murder. Therefore, McGimpsey said that the RUC should be involved in the murder inquiry.

The controversy over RUC involvement in the Nelson murder inquiry was further fuelled when Sir Ronnie Flanagan responded to a report that RUC officers had been investigated over making alleged death threats to Rosemary Nelson and no disciplinary action had been required. The RUC Chief Constable stated, 'Those officers have rights just in the way that everyone else has rights.' This was undoubtedly true, but this only intensified the desire among many to have the RUC completely removed from the inquiry into Rosemary's murder. The question remains as to why officers under investigation were not suspended.

A balanced view is needed here. The RUC, vastly unpopular among the Catholic/Republican community, could do no right, and its job had always been a very difficult one, policing a territory rife with political tensions and sectarian hatreds, as we have seen. However, the fact that officers under investigation were not removed from active duty while they were proved either innocent or guilty was at the very least a public relations catastrophe.

The Metropolitan Police had by now passed over its investigation report into the alleged death threats made against Rosemary Nelson to the DPP. This also covered an examination of the methods of the RUC investigation into the alleged death threats by members of its own organisation, although no official inquiry had taken place into the original RUC investigation. This truly was a Russian *babushka* doll of alleged collusion: every new, smaller doll seemed to give rise to more questions about alleged wrongdoing. On the same day, it was reported that the FBI was undertaking interviews with potential witnesses in Lurgan about Rosemary's murder but, as the Pat Finucane Centre later pointed out, nobody in Lurgan could confirm this fact.

On 27 March, more than 130 community groups placed an advert in the *Irish News* demanding an independent inquiry into Rosemary Nelson's death. Archbishop Sean Brady, the Catholic Primate of Ireland, backed this up the next day when he said, 'I would prefer the United Nations Special Rapporteur involved. I think it is important that it inspires confidence and I think it may be better if the RUC were out of the investigation altogether. They may have to provide back-up.'

The *Irish News* also ran a news report on 27 March showing that the mistrust of the RUC was not just confined to the Republican community. An inquest had just finished on the murder of a Loyalist called John McColgan, killed in January 1998. His widow said in the article that 'absolutely nothing' was actively under way to investigate his murder. His family also questioned why the RUC had not set up roadblocks on the day of McColgan's murder, even though his killers were driving his car. Also, why the RUC had been very slow in arriving at the murder scene and why the RUC had not contacted them for more than a year, despite the RUC claiming that it had been in contact.

On 28 March, the Irish Rights group Cearta ('*cearta*' is the Irish word for 'rights') organised a Sunday vigil for Rosemary Nelson at Belfast City Hall, and a few hundred people attended. The depth of outrage and feeling about her murder was not dying out, and neither would the attacks on the conduct of the RUC or indeed the British Government.

On that same day, *Ireland on Sunday* ran a piece claiming senior members of the RUC had attempted to influence the ICPC report into the way the RUC had dealt with the alleged death threats and abuses directed at Rosemary Nelson. Quoting legal sources, the newspaper reported that the RUC had tried, over a number of months, to convince the ICPC to 'tone down' and extract some of the criticisms made against the RUC. Also covered were the criticisms made by Param Cumaraswamy, the UN Special Rapporteur, whose follow-up report on Rosemary's case had just been finished, and was highly critical of both the British Government and the RUC. The UN report stated that the RUC Chief Constable Sir Ronnie Flanagan was guilty of 'allowing the situation to deteriorate' and that the RUC had shown 'complete indifference' to allegations made by defence lawyers, including Rosemary Nelson, that they had been threatened.

Exactly two weeks after Rosemary's murder, on 29 March, the British Government responded to mounting pressure and appointed Colin Port, the Deputy Chief Constable of Norfolk, to take 'day-to-day control, direction and command' of the Nelson murder inquiry. Colin Port had some experience of such investigations, having already been part of fully independent international investigations in the former Yugoslavia and Rwanda. However, Sir Ronnie Flanagan reiterated that the RUC would carry out the inquiry.

The RUC controversy raged on. The next day, Sir Ronnie Flanagan and Paul Donnelly, Chairman of the ICPC, made a statement about the investigation undertaken into alleged death threats against Rosemary Nelson. At the same time, Commander Niall Mulvihill released a ten-page summary report, expressing his views of the ICPC report. This led to some Republicans and human rights groups calling this report by Mulvihill an 'exercise in damage limitation' and others to claim that it was an attempt to dilute the validity of the ICPC report. The SDLP Assembly member Brid Rodgers challenged Sir

Ronnie Flanagan 'to accept the reality that the assessment of an independent supervisor from the ICPC is more objective and credible in the eyes of the community than that of a policeman'.

The very next day, the President of the Law Society of Northern Ireland said that its members would take no side in whether there should be an independent judicial inquiry into the murder of defence lawyer Pat Finucane ten years earlier. This upset many lawyers in Northern Ireland and elsewhere.

On 3 April, the *Andersonstown News* reported that the RUC had made an appeal for information about sightings of vehicles in and around Lurgan the day before the murder of Rosemary Nelson. They had faxed this out, but had used the wrong date for the day before Rosemary's murder. Naturally, this would compromise the reliability of any information supplied. Second, when a journalist on the newspaper tried to call the appeal number, there was a voicemail stating that the number was no longer in existence. This was less than three weeks after Rosemary's murder.

Nine days later, on 12 April, the UN Special Rapporteur Param Cumaraswamy provided his second report to the United Nations Commission on Human Rights. The claim made in *Ireland on Sunday* about the 'complete indifference' of the RUC regarding RUC harassment of lawyers was indeed in the report. In response, RUC Chief Constable Sir Ronnie Flanagan said, 'I reject the notion that we are indifferent. We are not indifferent. I take, and this organisation takes, any complaint very seriously indeed.' He went on to mention that he had brought in audio recording into RUC interviews and had asked the Law Society how his organisation could be 'fully sensitive to the role of defence lawyers'.

Pat Armstrong, Chairman of the Police Authority, supports Flanagan, denying Cumaraswamy's RUC 'indifference' claims.

The UN Special Rapporteur's report also claimed it had '*prima facie* evidence' of military and/or RUC collusion in the murder of Pat Finucane in 1989.

In response to the UN report, Brid Rodgers of the SDLP said, 'How many more internationally respected figures have to investigate his force before Mr Flanagan takes on board their criticism and does something to address their concerns?' Added to this, Martin O'Brien of the CAJ said, 'For a country which purports to uphold the rule of law and to have an international reputation for doing so, it is impossible the Government won't now establish an inquiry.'

Meanwhile, the RUC, the FBI's John Guido and Deputy Chief Constable of Norfolk Colin Port held a press conference. Port said, 'I am aware of reports that some members of the community who may have crucial information have made statements and disclosures to a number of organisations but have been reluctant to contact the police.' He asked anyone with information to come forward to the police, and stated in response to criticisms of RUC involvement in the Nelson murder inquiry that it would be 'severely handicapped' if the RUC was not involved in it.

John Guido of the FBI also supported the RUC. 'Frankly, we found the RUC to be well prepared to handle this investigation and we found little that we suggest they change or do differently.' Adam Ingram, the Security Minister, also backed Sir Ronnie Flanagan's efforts and RUC involvement in the murder investigation.

The next day, the RUC stated that the number of external participants was 'increasing every day' and that the murder inquiry consisted of 40 RUC officers and 10 English officers.

On 14 April, there was further international pressure exerted on the British Government. Probably in response to the UN Special Rapporteur Param Cumaraswamy's second report, the House International Relations Committee of the US Congress voted with its feet. It passed a motion stopping all funding for dual FBI/RUC training programmes until independent investigations into the murders of Rosemary Nelson and Pat Finucane were implemented. This was a major statement and would have a major political effect. In addition, Liz O'Donnell, the Irish Junior Minister of State for Foreign Affairs, in a letter to Dr Mo Mowlam called on the British Government to start a public inquiry into Pat Finucane's 1989 murder. On that same day, Dr Mowlam met up with Param Cumaraswamy and they both said that they would keep channels open between them. Cumaraswamy would also meet Chris Patten of the Independent Commission into Policing soon after.

The international pressure was reaching a crescendo now. The following day, the European Parliament passed a motion demanding a judicial inquiry and independent investigation into Rosemary's Nelson's murder. This was also echoed in Canada; the Canadian Bar Association, the Advocates' Society, the Law Society of Upper

Canada, the Law Union of Ontario and the Criminal Lawyers' Association all pressed for an international independent inquiry into Rosemary's murder. Meanwhile, remembrance services were held in Ireland, Britain, the USA, Australia, Canada and South Africa exactly a month after the murder.

On 19 April, there was a major new development in highlighting Rosemary's case: the Rosemary Nelson Campaign was set up in Belfast. The main drive of the campaign was to push for a fully independent judicial inquiry into Rosemary's murder and to fight to protect human rights in Northern Ireland, the cause which Rosemary had striven for. Dr Robbie McVeigh, spokesman for the Campaign, said, 'The murder of Rosemary Nelson was, of course, a terrible event with potentially huge implications for policing and human rights in the north of Ireland... Justice must be done and must be seen to be done in this case. If the RUC or other security forces were involved in collusion in the murder, then this must be exposed. If not, they have nothing to fear from an independent investigation and indeed should welcome it.'

The British human rights lawyer Gareth Pierce added, 'For that lawyer to be subjected to threats – or, far, far worse, a risk of assassination – is terrifying and destabilising.'

The following day, a human rights award was given posthumously to Rosemary Nelson. Backed by *The Times* and the human rights group JUSTICE, it is awarded to lawyers who make a considerable contribution to the struggle for human rights. It was presented to Rosemary's widower Paul Nelson, who accepted it on behalf of his late wife.

That same day in the United States, the US House of Representatives passed a resolution demanding a fully independent investigation – that specifically excluded the RUC – into Rosemary's murder and for an independent judicial inquiry into the allegations made by lawyers of intimidation by the security forces. Congressman Chris Smith said, 'For far too long, the people of Northern Ireland have lived in fear of their own police force. It is incumbent on that force to step aside from this investigation, and allow a fair and impartial investigation, if for no other reason to prove that they have nothing to hide.' These were strong and direct words from the highly powerful and internationally influential US Congress.

That evening, a BBC *Spotlight* programme focusing on Rosemary's murder said that there were now no less than six English police constabularies taking part in the murder investigation. It also stated that the explosive used in the bomb under Rosemary's car had not been powergel as originally believed, and that the Red Hand Defenders, who had claimed responsibility for the act, was the same organisation as that known as the Orange Volunteers, but under a different name. Of course, as we have seen, the LVF was actually behind both dissident splinter groups.

The pressure for an independent inquiry was now relentless. On 21 April, the Rosemary Nelson Campaign placed a prominent, full-page advertisement in the *Irish Times* in the form of an open letter addressed to the Irish Taoiseach Bertie Ahern. The thrust of the letter was to compel Ahern to support the demand for an international and independent judicial inquiry into Rosemary's murder 'in deed and word' and included a coupon for readers to cut out, fill in and send to Ahern to lobby him. Ahern said in the Dail, the Irish Parliament, that day that the allegations of intimidation and harassment made against the RUC 'are of more than merit'. Ahern added, 'We have to try and negotiate with the British Government and be satisfied – which we are not yet, but I hope we will be – that the investigation is operated in such a way that all potential witnesses can with confidence come forward. If we can achieve that I will be happy – if we can't, then we will have to look further.'

On 22 April 1999, five weeks after her murder, Rosemary had been scheduled to give evidence before the House International Relations Committee of the US Congress in Washington, DC. The Chairman of that Committee, US Congressman Ben Gilman, was chairing hearings focused on the RUC. The sister of the murdered Robert Hamill, Diana Hamill, gave evidence, and Dr Robbie McVeigh represented the Rosemary Nelson Campaign. A statement provided by Paul Nelson was read on his behalf for the benefit of the Congressional Record. As this statement was written by the person closest to the late Rosemary Nelson, and allows us to see his grave concerns, it is worth quoting in full here. This was Paul Nelson's statement:

'This is obviously a difficult and painful time for our family. We have been helped by the sympathy and support shown by the international community. Not least in this has been the support of members of Congress for the two requests made by us following Rosemary's murder – for a fully independent

international investigation and an independent international judicial inquiry into the circumstances surrounding Rosemary's death.

'These requests now constitute the key objectives of the Rosemary Nelson Campaign. The Campaign brings together members of Rosemary's family, her friends, lawyers and human rights activists who each have a commitment to truth and justice for Rosemary. Human rights lawyers are in the front line of the defence of human rights around the world. In this context the murder of Rosemary was a direct and profound attack on the human rights of everybody in Ireland and beyond. Swift movement towards the establishment of a fully independent international investigation and inquiry into the circumstances surrounding Rosemary's death is necessary to ensure that the human rights, which were guaranteed by the Good Friday Agreement, can be properly protected.

'The murder of Rosemary was a terrible event with potentially huge implications for policing and human rights in the north of Ireland. It was, however, primarily a human tragedy for her family and friends. Whatever happens in terms of the pursuit of truth and justice in this case, it bears emphasis that our loss can never be replaced. It is also true, however, that there will be some solace for our family in the achievement of the truth about the circumstances surrounding her murder.

'This is why the Rosemary Nelson Campaign focuses on two fairly simple and palpably reasonable demands: (1) an independent international

investigation; and (2) an independent judicial inquiry. These are the only mechanisms capable of securing the truth so desperately demanded by her family, her friends and the wider community.

'*Rosemary was consistently and routinely death-threatened by members of the RUC. She was subsequently murdered. Justice must be done and must be seen to be done in this case. If the RUC or other security forces were involved in collusion in the murder, this must be exposed. If they were not, they have nothing to fear from any independent investigation and, indeed, they should welcome it. If there was security force collusion in the murder of Rosemary, then culpability for that collusion sits not only with the RUC but with the British Government.*

'*The UN Basic Principles on the Role of Lawyers make clear that it is not enough for a government to adopt a policy of non-interference with lawyers. The duty goes much further – it is a positive duty – as Principle 16 provides: "Governments shall ensure that lawyers are able to perform all of their professional functions without intimidation, hindrance, harassment or improper interference." There is no greater intimidation to all lawyers than the death of a high-profile human rights lawyer. A fully independent investigation and inquiry is needed for governments to live up to United Nations obligations. From this perspective, it is in the interests of the British Government to move quickly to support an independent inquiry and investigation. The Secretary of State and the Prime Minister have a*

*clear interest and duty to ensure that this case is dealt
with quickly and appropriately.*

'Furthermore, Principle 18 of the UN Basic
Principles on the Role of Lawyers provides that:
"Lawyers shall not be identified with their clients or
their clients' causes as a result of discharging their
functions." This principle underwrites the
independence of lawyers which is a necessary part of
the right to a fair trial that all suspects should
possess in any democratic society, and to which the
Government has committed itself as a signatory of
human rights conventions such as the European
Convention on Human Rights. Human rights
lawyers are in the front line of the defence of human
rights around the world. This is why Rosemary's
death has so shocked the international human rights
community. It is also the key to understanding why
the campaign will and must be a success.*

'If we are to have human rights in Northern
Ireland, then there can be no place for the
harassment of defence lawyers, there can be no place
for the death-threatening of defence lawyers, and
there can be no place for the murder of defence
lawyers. The international human rights community
understands this and will be a key part of the alliance
to secure truth and justice for Rosemary.*

'Rosemary's work was, on the one hand, that of an
ordinary solicitor serving all communities in Lurgan
and beyond. But her commitment to a whole range
of human rights work marked her out as a human
rights defender in the widest sense. One of the most
common tributes that have been paid to her is that*

she would work for anyone from any community, regardless of their religion or politics. That is the true mark of a human rights lawyer.

'We ask Congress to do its utmost to support our aim – truth and justice for Rosemary. We also ask you to support our two objectives – an independent international investigation and an independent international judicial inquiry into the circumstances surrounding her death. We cannot overestimate the importance of the continued support of Congress for these objectives. We obviously hope that both of these objectives will be realised swiftly. But we also commit ourselves to campaign for these objectives for as long as it takes. To do any less would be to do a disservice to the cause of human rights which Rosemary so ably and committedly served.

'Thank you for your continuing sympathy and support.'

7

THE AMERICAN ANGLE

The connection between Ireland and the United States has always been a strong one, both spiritually and politically. Masses of Irish men and women emigrated to 'the New World' in the late nineteenth and early twentieth century for a better life, often escaping great hardship and sometimes starvation. The acceleration of the struggles in Northern Ireland in the latter half of the twentieth century was keenly watched on the other side of the Atlantic, and it is no secret that Republican coffers were long replenished by Irish-American donations.

There are also questions to be asked why both the United States and Britain maintained strong interest in Northern Ireland, despite the political headache caused by the Troubles, particularly from the late 1960s until the early 1990s. It is true that there was a majority consensus in Northern Ireland fuelled by the Protestant population that it should remain part of Britain, but everybody knows that high-level political decisions are not always made because they have a mandate with a public majority or a significant minority. If Britain could have ridded itself of the burden of Northern Ireland, it probably would have done.

The special relationship between Britain and the United States in the Second World War is of importance here. Frankly, Northern Ireland was of little economic interest to either power, its GDP and export potential being small fry. But perhaps it was of territorial interest; these were the darkest days of the Cold War, when the threat came from the Soviet Union. Could Northern Ireland have been seen as of strategic importance against the Soviet Union, especially in lending a capacity to land and launch aircraft, and for the use of her deep sea ports for access to the Baltic Sea where Russian submarines operated?

Speaking off the record, an Irishman with a very good knowledge of the political complexities of Northern Ireland told one of the authors, Neil Root, his opinion of the main reason that the peace process did not pick up speed until the mid-1990s. It was then that both Britain and the United States began applying real pressure for that to happen. Why did it only happen then? Could it be that, by then, the Soviet Union had collapsed, and was no longer a threat to Britain and the US, so Northern Ireland was no longer of strategic importance?

The same source told the authors about rumoured allegations within Ireland (which cannot be substantiated) that Knock Airport in the west of Ireland, which opened in 1986, had been built with the aid of CIA funding, and that such clandestine funding from the US ran deep. Although a commercial airport today, as recently as 2007, Knock Airport was reportedly being considered as a refuelling stop for US military transport planes, a role that Shannon Airport already performs. However, confirmation of this angle will only be possible in the course of time when records become available – provided, of course, that key information has not been discarded or redacted.

The murder of Rosemary Nelson was an atrocity of great interest and indignation in the United States, and the powerful House of Congress exerted much influence on the case in the months and years that followed. This influence should not be underestimated and gave the case an international reach. Two days before Paul Nelson's statement was read out to Congress, that institution passed a House Resolution, the prime sponsor being Republican Congressman Mr Christopher H Smith of New Jersey. House Resolution 128 was titled 'Condemning the Murder of Northern Ireland Human Rights Attorney Rosemary Nelson'. This was the foundation stone of American political reaction to Rosemary Nelson's murder and so was the beginning of political pressure to see justice done on her behalf and for the sake of human rights in Northern Ireland, coming from the most powerful country in the world.

The Resolution opened with a reminder of Rosemary Nelson's claims that she had been 'physically assaulted by a number of RUC officers' and that her problems with the RUC were 'at their most serious, making threats against my personal safety including death threats'. Rosemary had, of course, told the Subcommittee on International Operations and Human Rights of the US Congress this herself directly when she testified before it on 29 September 1998, six-and-a-half months before her murder.

House Resolution 128, heard just over a month after her murder, also focused on the findings of the UN Special Rapporteur Param Cumaraswamy, whose investigation into alleged harassment by individual officers within the RUC of defence lawyers in Northern Ireland had found that 'these harassments and intimidation were consistent and systematic'. The Congress also heard how the UN Special Rapporteur had recommended 'an independent and impartial investigation of all threats to legal counsel in Northern Ireland', and that 'where there is a threat to the physical integrity of a solicitor, the Government should provide necessary protection'. The Resolution then went on to quote from the ICPC's report into the RUC investigation of the alleged threats against Rosemary. It reminded Congress that it had found the RUC 'hostile, evasive and disinterested', and had noticed an 'ill-disguised hostility to Mrs Nelson on the part of some police officers'.

Next, the focus shifted to the fact that the British Government 'provided protection for Northern Ireland judges after paramilitary violence resulted in the death of four judges and some family members', and then stipulated that the British Government 'should also provide appropriate protection for defence attorneys'. It then paid tribute to Rosemary Nelson, the mother of three children, who, although she faced death threats and intimidation, 'courageously continued to represent the rights of Catholic clients in high-profile cases', citing her representation of the GRRC and the family of Robert Hamill.

Rosemary Nelson's murder itself came next, with a call that 'all those involved in the targeting and killing... including the Red Hand Defenders... must be brought to justice'. The Resolution also pointed out that 'the success of the peace process is predicated on the ability of the people of Northern Ireland to believe that injustices such as the murder of Rosemary Nelson will be investigated thoroughly, fairly, and transparently'. This was a key point, as the hearts and minds of the people of Northern Ireland, on both sides of the sectarian divide, could not, of course, be won over unless there was solid trust in unbiased and transparent justice. The reluctance of potential witnesses in Lurgan to come forward to the RUC with information about Rosemary's murder illustrates this point.

As we have seen, the parallels between the murders of Pat Finucane and Rosemary Nelson are striking, and they began to be raised, especially as a decade after Finucane's murder no independent inquiry had taken place. Congress House Resolution 128 stated that the UN report also said that 'since the Patrick Finucane murder, further information that seriously calls into question whether there was official collusion has come to light'. This will be examined more fully later.

Resolution 128 closed by making five resolutions: (i) that Congress fully supported the Northern Ireland Peace Process; (ii) all violence was condemned; (iii) it called on the British Government to instigate an independent, public inquiry into Rosemary Nelson's murder 'not connected to or reliant upon the efforts of the Royal Ulster Constabulary (RUC)'; (iv) to start an independent judicial inquiry of alleged harassment and intimidation of defence lawyers by security forces; and (v) to launch an independent inquiry into the 1989 Pat Finucane murder, as recommended by the UN Special Rapporteur in his report.

This was the first official American action in the aftermath of Rosemary Nelson's murder, but there had been an American involvement through human rights co-operation in the years leading up to it. The New York City Bar was consistently active in fostering relations with Northern Ireland, sending two 'Missions' in 1987 and 1998 (a third visited in 2003), as well as Northern Ireland delegations visiting New York.

The 1987 Mission consisted of three delegates from the New York City Bar. They met with a wide range of law-enforcement and legal representatives including senior members of the RUC, judges and defence solicitors and barristers (but not Rosemary Nelson, as she had yet to set up her own practice). By that time, 2,500 people had been killed in the Troubles since 1969. Since 1972, the Irish Parliament had been suspended, and rule came directly from London. The delegation witnessed police and army patrols, checkpoints and roadblocks as well as walls built to segregate Protestant and Catholic areas.

It was a form of religious/political apartheid, with the RUC having powers of arrest, interrogation and detention and non-jury trials for terrorist suspects seen nowhere else in Britain, an extended remit of powers which Rosemary Nelson would come to know so well. Of course, it should also be remembered that the Troubles in Northern Ireland were like nothing else faced by Britain, too – they were extreme measures in an extreme situation. However, the curbing of human rights for suspects was disturbing in a legal system overseen from the Westminster Parliament, the oldest democracy in the world, and one that has always prided itself on its liberal freedoms and tolerant approach. But some would argue that it was a war, and wartime always requires the use of exceptional measures.

The New York City Bar was critical of the British Government after this visit, as their 2009 report *Human Rights in Action* makes clear. Its main concern was that these emergency legal laws and powers had gone on for so long that they were becoming permanently ingrained, allowing erosion of human rights in Northern Ireland. One of the delegates on the 1987 Mission was William E Hellerstein, now a Professor of Law at Brooklyn Law School, and, in 2009, he referred to his 1987 visit to Northern Ireland as 'one of the outstanding experiences of my professional life'. The report and recommendations for the promotion of peace and human rights in Northern Ireland was covered by the *New York Times* and a copy of the report was given to then Prime Minister Margaret Thatcher's office, getting 'positive responses'.

However, the next Mission undertaken by the New York City Bar to Northern Ireland in October 1998 showed that these human rights abuses were still explicit.

Two years after the 1987 Mission, in 1989, the defence lawyer Pat Finucane was gunned down in his home by Loyalists. As the 2009 New York Bar report makes clear, Finucane 'had been the target of threats by RUC officers who transmitted the threats to his clients during interrogations'. Similarly, certain clients of Rosemary Nelson are alleged to have reported threats to her said to be from RUC officers just a few years later.

During the October 1998 Mission, Rosemary Nelson told the American delegates of her concerns for the safety of defence lawyers and for herself and her family, as we have seen. This was just six months before her murder.

Also on that Mission, the New York City Bar called for a full judicial inquiry into Finucane's murder, as the 2009 report states 'in light of the substantial and credible evidence pointing to collusion by the security forces with the paramilitaries responsible for Finucane's murder'. This was almost a decade after Finucane's murder, and there still had not been an independent, public inquiry.

The American Bar Association (ABA), which then had 400,000 members, was also involved in calling for justice in the Rosemary Nelson case. On 29 July 1999, Philip S Anderson, the President of the ABA, wrote to the Secretary of State for Northern Ireland, Dr Mo Mowlam. Copies of the letter also went to, among others, US Secretary of State Madeleine Albright, Taoiseach Bertie Ahern and Christopher Meyer, then British Ambassador to the United States. He opened his letter with: 'I write to convey our serious concerns regarding alleged violations of human rights occurring in Northern Ireland. We are particularly concerned about the investigation into the murder of human rights lawyer, Rosemary Nelson.'

The ABA President referred to the UN Special Rapporteur's report and those of human rights organisations that RUC officers 'have engaged in systematic abuse of defence lawyers in Northern Ireland'. He went on to cite the complaints that Rosemary Nelson herself had made about alleged threats to her safety and alleged death threats reported to her by certain of her clients from the RUC when she testified before the US Congress in September 1998. Anderson also made reference to the UN Special Rapporteur's report regarding the abuse of rights of suspects arrested and detained in Northern Ireland. These were: the right to access to counsel during interrogation; the right to remain silent; the right to be free from use of confessions that were secured by psychological pressure, deprivation or other non-violent forms of coercion; and the right to trial by jury. The ABA President urged the British Government through Mo Mowlam to address these alleged human rights abuses.

Anderson then focused on RUC involvement in the Nelson murder inquiry, saying that the investigation 'should be performed by an authority independent of the RUC in order for it to have credibility within the national and international legal and human rights communities'. He strengthened this by writing that 'the Government's concern for security should not justify abrogation of fundamental rights of fair criminal procedure'.

On 14 March 2000, Paul Mageean, now Director of Studies of the Graduate School for Professional Legal Education at the University of Ulster, gave testimony representing the CAJ at the Helsinki Commission Hearing of the United States Commission on Security and Co-operation in Europe. Mageean had also testified, along with Rosemary Nelson, before the House International Relations Committee Hearing on Human Rights in Northern Ireland on 29 September 1998. In his new testimony, Mageean shared his knowledge of Rosemary Nelson's case, a day short of the first anniversary of her murder.

Paul Mageean refreshed the memory of the CAJ about the alleged threats made against Rosemary by the RUC reported to her by certain of her clients, two specific written threats she had received, and her great concern at how those threats were investigated. Mr Mageean also stated, 'I will also try to indicate ways in which the United States Government can assist in ensuring that the investigation into Rosemary's murder is carried out in an independent and effective fashion.'

Mageean recounted how, on 10 August 1998, he and Rosemary Nelson had written to Adam Ingram, then Minister of Security at the NIO, enclosing two documents to illustrate their concern about the threats made to her. Both of these threats have been recounted already in this book: the first was the note calling Rosemary a 'republican bastard... RIP', and the other was the pamphlet threatening Breandan Mac Cionnaith, the leader of the GRRC, called *The Man Without a Future*. It might be recalled that this pamphlet also made it clear that Rosemary Nelson had given legal advice to Mac Cionnaith, and that her address and telephone contact details were printed in the pamphlet.

Regarding these threats, Mageean told the CAJ, 'We said in our letter that we considered these documents to be very definite threats against Rosemary Nelson and told Mr Ingram that we considered it incumbent on the Government to investigate these matters and also to provide the necessary protection for Rosemary.'

The reply from Adam Ingram's office came six weeks later. It read: 'Obviously, the documents enclosed must be of concern to Ms Nelson and the others mentioned. The Minister has asked me to say that he hopes that those who produced them can be brought to justice for their threatening behaviour.'

The threats had also been given to the Chief Constable of the RUC, Sir Ronnie Flanagan, and the letter from Ingram's office said that the RUC would investigate them, making an assessment of the risk against Rosemary Nelson. It also informed Rosemary and Mageean that Rosemary could put in for security measures to be fitted at her home at taxpayers' expense through the Key Persons Protection Scheme (KPPS). But as Paul Mageean told the US Congress Commission, 'Rosemary did not do this as it would have entailed RUC officers carrying out security checks on her home. It was, of course, officers from this force whom she believed were issuing threats against her.' As we shall see, this would become all the more ironic long after Rosemary Nelson's murder, when the question arose of whether her home had been bugged by individual officers from the RUC.

Mageean also pointed out in his testimony that, after Rosemary's murder, the RUC contacted the CAJ (of which Mageean was the legal officer), asking for the originals of the threat documents, as they wanted to try to lift fingerprints from them. The CAJ no longer had the originals but, as Mageean said to the Congress Commission, why had they not asked for the threat documents when they were told about them, a full seven months before Rosemary Nelson was murdered? Mageean said, 'Surely it would have been a basic investigative step to seek the originals of the documents when they received them rather than wait until after the target of the threats was murdered.'

The CAJ did not leave it there, as Paul Mageean explained in his testimony. It wrote to the RUC's Chief Constable on 3 June 1999, asking for answers to questions regarding the RUC's response to the threats before Rosemary's murder. Sir Ronnie Flanagan acknowledged this letter eight days later, but did not follow up. So the CAJ sent another letter on 30 July, and there was no response to this either. The CAJ finally met with Flanagan on 4 October 1999, at which meeting he promised to deal with its questions in writing. This, too, was not forthcoming, according to Mageean in his testimony, and the CAJ then wrote several reminders that also elicited no response. The CAJ sent a final letter to Flanagan on 9 March 2000, informing him that Mageean would be testifying before the Commission on Security and Co-operation in Europe in the US on 14 March, five days later. This did get a response from Flanagan, on the day of the testimony.

Sir Ronnie Flanagan's letter read: 'In connection with your letter of 3 June 1999 specifically relating to the murder of Mrs Nelson, I explained to you at our meeting that the RUC itself had no intelligence prior to Mrs Nelson's death to indicate a threat of the dreadful atrocity which was to be carried out.' He went on to say that it was not 'appropriate to discuss the details you raise while the investigation is current', and mentioned Colin Port, Deputy Chief Constable of Norfolk, who was now overseeing the Rosemary Nelson murder investigation.

Paul Mageean's main thrust in his testimony that day was to question the RUC's prevarication in investigating the threats against Rosemary Nelson until after her murder, and he said that he found Sir Ronnie Flanagan's letter unsatisfactory. Mageean stated, 'In CAJ's view, this response does not address our key concern, namely the apparent inaction of the police between August 1998 (when they were informed of the death threats) and Mrs Nelson's subsequent murder in March 1999. It was only after Mrs Nelson's death that the police showed evident signs of the threats being taken seriously.' He went on to request the Commission on Security and Co-operation in Europe to write to the British Government, asking why they had not followed up the threats immediately by seeking the originals of the documents, seven months before Rosemary Nelson's murder.

Paul Mageean added, 'We believe that the police and the Government have not answered our questions in this regard because they are unable to provide an adequate answer. We believe the police failed to carry out an adequate assessment of the risk against Rosemary Nelson. We believe their failures in relation to that assessment are emblematic of their failure to investigate the ongoing threats against Rosemary by their own members.'

On the same day as the testimony, the *Irish News* carried an interview with the UN Special Rapporteur Param Cumaraswamy, in which he said that he had asked the British Government to give protection to Rosemary Nelson. In the article, he asked the Government directly, 'You tell us. You knew about it. What did you do?' Mageean quoted this, before referring to the report made by the ICPC commissioned by the British Government to investigate the complaints made by Rosemary Nelson of abuse and threats. Mageean stated that the ICPC was 'not satisfied with the RUC investigation', as we saw earlier. He also spoke about the view within the RUC that the pressure being put on it by 'international groups on behalf of Mrs Nelson' was a political move and 'more to do with propaganda against the RUC than establishing the truth'. Mageean then compared this with the findings of the English policeman Commander Niall Mulvihill, who 'expressed satisfaction with the conduct of the investigation'. To this, the ICPC Chairperson Paul Donnelly had responded that Mulvihill's report was based on 'assertions, conclusions and recommendations that rely heavily on impression and belief, as opposed to systematically testable evidence'.

Paul Mageean then told the Commission that a senior member of the ICPC itself, a female lawyer, had been threatened and had become 'the subject of a whispering campaign by police officers and members of the policing establishment which questioned her impartiality and ability'. This had happened after the publication of the ICPC report, and had forced the female lawyer to move house.

The focus was then on the conduct and results of the Rosemary Nelson murder inquiry, now led by Colin Port, Deputy Chief Constable of Norfolk Constabulary. Mageean testified that, on 9 March 2000, almost a year after the murder, the first two arrests had been made, but one suspect had already been released. The man still being held on the day of testimony on 14 March was reportedly a 'serving soldier at the time of Rosemary's murder'. As we shall see, Sir Ronnie Flanagan, Chief Constable of the RUC, would later say that he knew who the Nelson bombing team were, although he did not give a date as to when he first knew this.

Mageean also said that Port was also investigating possible collusion in Rosemary's murder, although 'he has also indicated that to date the collusion enquiries have not yielded any results'. In his testimony, Paul Mageean stated that the CAJ 'remain concerned that Mr Port continues to conduct his investigation from Lurgan RUC station'. He went on to say that the 'continuing involvement' of the RUC in the Nelson murder inquiry was 'undermining confidence' in the inquiry's independence, with the result that potential witnesses were not coming forward.

Representing the CAJ, Mageean followed this by testifying that he had little faith in the murder investigation, saying, 'it is apparent that the criminal investigation, even if successfully concluded, will not result in a full examination of the circumstances surrounding the murder of Rosemary Nelson'. He also alluded to the 'heavy security presence' in the vicinity of her home prior to her murder that needed to be investigated. Next he called for a full public and completely independent inquiry into Rosemary's murder, citing the support for this from the United Nations, Amnesty International, the Lawyers Committee for Human Rights and Human Rights Watch. His assertion was that in any democratic country such a step would be taken, and that the British Government should act no differently. He added that the CAJ 'believe the failure to establish such an inquiry is a violation of the United Kingdom's international obligation to make available effective remedies for the violation of human rights'.

Paul Mageean concluded his testimony to the Commission on Security and Co-operation in Europe by saying, 'Rosemary Nelson was a member of the Executive Committee of CAJ. She dedicated her professional life to obtaining justice for others. We will do all we can to obtain justice for her.'

The American concern about alleged State RUC collusion in Rosemary Nelson's murder was shown to have reached the very highest level in a leaked memo from President George W Bush to Colin Powell, the Secretary of State on 7 December 2001.

The RUC had recently been abolished, to make way for the new PSNI, and the leaked memo concerned the training of new PSNI officers. There had been a ban imposed by the US Congress in relation to the FBI training the RUC because of a perceived Protestant bias within the RUC. To lift the ban, a special certification memorandum was required from the US President. But in mid-January 2002, President Bush's Special Envoy to Northern Ireland, Richard Haass, announced that the new PSNI was welcome to send police officers to be trained at the FBI training academy at Quantico (the training would also include human rights protocol). This was obviously a move to give support to the fledgling PSNI, a show of co-operation in a new era.

However, Richard Haass made no mention of access restrictions to the PSNI when he made his announcement at a press conference. But President Bush's leaked memo to Secretary of State Colin Powell did mention such restrictions, namely, the PSNI officers to be trained at Quantico would be closely vetted. Bush's memo read:

'Vetting procedures have been established in the Departments of State and Justice, and any other appropriate Federal agency to ensure that training or exchange programs do not include PSNI members who there are substantial grounds for believing have committed or condoned violations of internationally recognized human rights, including any role in the murder of Patrick Finucane or

Rosemary Nelson or other violence against defense attorneys in Northern Ireland.'

This was a very significant admission from the US President that his administration did have grave concerns about alleged RUC involvement in the shooting of Finucane in February 1989 and the car bombing of Rosemary Nelson in March 1999. The fact that Mr Bush intervened and felt it necessary to stipulate that the training would exclude any former RUC officer who had any possible alleged link to either murder shows that these suspicions and concerns were prominent at the very highest level. It also indicates a fear that would continue to fester within Northern Ireland – the RUC was no more, but would the PSNI be tainted by suspicions – well founded or not – over the behaviour of former RUC members?

The policing body had a new name and new procedures but, in the minds of many, the tumour of suspicion concerning the question of State collusion had not been fully removed.

On 29 December 2005, the award-winning US human rights attorney Edmund Lynch gave an interview to the *Daily Ireland*. Lynch, who knew Rosemary Nelson, explained how he had been on his way to a White House St Patrick's Day reception at the invitation of President Bill Clinton and the First Lady Hillary Clinton when he first heard the news about Rosemary's murder. Lynch said, 'I, and many others, were in shock that Rosemary was killed when, for two years, we had been sounding the alarm that her life was in danger and she was in need of protection.' He then went on to list 17 key dates when the threats against Rosemary were being raised and the response from the British Government (the NIO and Northern Ireland Secretary Mo Mowlam) and the RUC. These dates were between 13 March 1997 and the day of Rosemary Nelson's murder, almost exactly two years later on 15 March 1999.

It is sobering reading when one realises that all of these warnings and opportunities for action, over two years, between highly prominent and powerful people internationally, did not prevent the bomb from exploding under Rosemary Nelson's BMW.

The main questions must be addressed to the British Government and the security services acting in its name. There appear to be only four alternative conclusions: alleged incompetence, alleged negligence, alleged collusion or unavoidable tragedy.

ARRESTS

By the middle of 2000, there were four suspects being considered by the Rosemary Nelson murder inquiry team led by Colin Port. Two of these were known veteran Loyalist gunmen; the other two had acted as informers for RUC Special Branch.

One was a serving army officer, a young soldier called Ian Thompson from the RIR (a regiment whose main purpose was counter-terrorism). Very soon after Rosemary's murder, Thompson left the RIR. When his home was searched, it was found to contain a poster of the late LVF Loyalist leader Billy Wright on a wall, as well as neo-Nazi material (Thompson was also found to have links to the neo-Nazi group Combat 18). In March 2001, Thompson appeared in a Belfast court charged with possession of illegal weapons: an Uzi machine-gun, a sawn-off shotgun and explosives. Some of the neo-Nazi material seized by the police also made specific references to Rosemary Nelson.

This evidence was put before the judge at Thompson's trial, Mr Justice McLaughlin. McLaughlin said that there was 'some material in these depositions that would make the blood run cold. There are remarks made about Rosemary Nelson which have no place in any decent society.' Ian Thompson was jailed for nine years, but continued to deny that he had been involved in surveying the area around Rosemary's home in the days before she was killed, a suspicion specifically put to him. It should be remembered here, as we have seen earlier, that RIR patrols on foot and in helicopters had been seen in the vicinity of Rosemary's Lurgan home as part of the unexplained 'security' presence in the days leading up to her murder.

The other suspect arrested was a Protestant preacher. The preacher had first been arrested in 1997 for storing hand grenades in his church, but he faced no prosecution. Late in 2000, his car was searched and a rocket launcher was found inside – this time he was prosecuted and given a ten-year sentence in 2001. The police who searched his home seized his computer and found documents relating to Rosemary Nelson on it.

On 29 November 2001, it was announced that the Rosemary Nelson murder inquiry team had arrested two men aged 29 and 60 near Portadown, and that two handguns and ammunition were found when they were arrested. These arrests will be examined in more detail later.

MURDER OF A JOURNALIST
28 September 2001, evening
Close to the Loyalist Mourneview Estate, Lurgan

Martin and Marie O'Hagan were walking back from a pub on Market Street in Lurgan, one frequented by both Loyalist and Republican customers. Fifty-one-year-old O'Hagan was a prominent investigative journalist on the Belfast tabloid the *Sunday World*, and no stranger to controversy. He was the journalist who had given the late UVF Commander and LVF leader Billy Wright the nickname 'King Rat' in the 1990s, and his cohorts the 'Rat Pack'. Both names stuck in the public consciousness, angering Wright and his followers, causing the LVF to bomb the *Sunday World* offices and triggering threats from Wright, as we have seen. O'Hagan and his colleagues on the newspaper had become used to threats from Loyalist paramilitaries, but saw it as a necessary hazard of their job – and their investigations into those same paramilitary groups weren't just in the context of sectarian violence, but increasingly involved alleged drug racketeering. The threats did not stop O'Hagan from going about his daily life, but he had started to take the precaution of varying his routes, especially when walking to and from the pub with his wife, as he was that evening.

O'Hagan's father was a soldier in the British Army, and Martin was born on an army base in Germany, but the family returned to Lurgan when he was seven, and Martin continued to live in the small town. When he was a teenager, O'Hagan had become involved in the military wing of the IRA (the Official IRA, before the Provisional IRA took over), as at that time he was attracted to its socialist politics. He was interned in the Maze in 1971

146

for a year and, soon after his release, he was sentenced to a further seven years for moving guns for the IRA, and was released in 1978.

O'Hagan began to hate the sectarian divisions in his native Northern Ireland and, in fact, his wife, Marie Dukes, was a Protestant (like his family, but a departure from his earlier IRA affiliation), and they went on to have three daughters together. O'Hagan kept his socialist leanings, and they were evident in his work for the *Sunday World* when he became a journalist. In 1989, O'Hagan was kidnapped and interrogated by the Provisional IRA about an article he had written, and this illustrates how his investigations were not confined to Loyalist paramilitaries. Much later, he also became the secretary of the Belfast branch of the National Union of Journalists.

O'Hagan had recently been left in no doubt that he was still a target. On another trip to the pub, he had been approached by a man on the street, a Loyalist, who told him that he had been 'clocked', slang for observed or spotted. That Friday evening of 28 September 2001, O'Hagan and his wife were on their way home to Westland Gardens in Lurgan when a car pulled up beside them, very close to their home.

O'Hagan reacted swiftly, pushing his wife Marie into a hedge as a gunman opened fire from the open car window. O'Hagan was hit several times, but he was able to ask Marie to call an ambulance. However, by the time it arrived, O'Hagan was dead.

The Red Hand Defenders claimed responsibility for the murder of Martin O'Hagan, the same Loyalist group that had claimed responsibility for Rosemary Nelson's murder. But it was widely known that it was a cover name for the LVF, and now led by Billy Wright's protégé, Mark Fulton, then locked up in Maghaberry Prison awaiting trial for conspiracy to murder rival Loyalist paramilitary members.

EXIT THE MASTERMIND
9 June 2002
Maghaberry Prison, County Antrim

Mark Fulton was a tortured man that night, a man who had possessed considerable paramilitary power as leader of the LVF. It was widely known that Fulton had never recovered from his hero and mentor Billy Wright's murder by the INLA inside the Maze Prison in 1997. But the torment and fear in Fulton's mind that night was mainly caused by more recent developments. Fulton had been ousted as the leader of the LVF, whose command structure had recently changed and the leadership taken over by another Belfast paramilitary group. Fulton knew that his days were numbered, but he did not fear Republican assassins, but those whom he had upset within his own Loyalist community. Fulton was old news and now disposable and he knew it, so much so that he had begged to be placed in isolation in the prison, along with his brother Jim. That was where he now resided, depressed and suicidal. Even letters in prison from his friend the notorious Loyalist Johnny 'Mad Dog' Adair could not snap him out of his depression.

When prison officers found him the next morning, Mark 'Swinger' Fulton, Loyalist, drug-dealer, killer and mastermind behind many prominent murders (allegedly 12 in all), including those of Rosemary Nelson and the journalist Martin O'Hagan, had a belt tied tightly

148

around his neck. He had committed suicide before they got to him. Foul play was quickly ruled out. Fulton's friend Johnny 'Mad Dog' Adair helped to carry his coffin at the funeral.

Within days of Fulton's suicide, police sources close to Colin Port, Deputy Chief Constable of Norfolk and leader of the Rosemary Nelson murder inquiry, named Mark Fulton as the brains behind Rosemary Nelson's murder. The sources were quoted in the *Sunday Herald* on 16 June 2002, saying that 'Fulton has long been the chief suspect... Although Fulton was in jail at the time of her death, we know how he planned and ordered it.' The sources went on to say that Fulton had been out of prison on compassionate leave only days before Rosemary's murder, and it was on the outside that he put the finishing touches to the plan to murder her. 'There is no question that he was the man who made this happen,' said a source. 'Fulton was linked to the killing through police informants, not through forensics. If there were any forensics, he'd have been serving life for her murder when he died.'

The sources then spoke about the team who actually made and planted the bomb that killed Rosemary Nelson, saying that it was believed that there had been a bomb-maker from Belfast, another person who delivered the bomb to the LVF, and two more who actually planted the bomb – including Fulton, a five-person team in all. The police source went on to say that the inquiry would continue until the whole team had been convicted for Rosemary's murder. However, Fulton's death meant that there could never be a confession from the planner.

So the assumed mastermind behind Rosemary Nelson's

murder was dead, by his own hand. The police investigating her murder believed they knew the make-up of the Nelson bombing team. But that still left the unanswered question of alleged State collusion in her murder, and it took an independent inquiry to start to answer this.

8

THE CORY COLLUSION INQUIRY

The mounting pressure within Northern Ireland, the United States and the United Nations, as well as seminal human rights organisations such as Amnesty International, put enormous pressure on the British Government to institute an independent judicial and public inquiry into Rosemary Nelson's murder. The voices of prominent and powerful people on the international stage, as well as the persistent work done by the Rosemary Nelson Campaign and the CAJ were not to go unheard. But the British Government did not opt directly for an independent, public inquiry. It first called an independent and eminent legal professional to conduct an inquiry into alleged State collusion in Rosemary Nelson's murder.

Judge Peter Cory, a retired Supreme Court of Canada puisne judge (1989–99) and a Companion of the Order of Canada (2002), was appointed to undertake the inquiry in 2003. As well as the Rosemary Nelson case, he was also requested to undertake collusion inquiries into the cases of Patrick Finucane, Billy Wright and Robert Hamill, all three of which have been outlined in this book.

It should also be noted that Judge Cory undertook collusion investigations into the 1989 murders of two RUC officers, Chief Superintendent Breen and Superintendent Buchanan, in a Provisional IRA ambush. He found that the evidence he gathered, which included intelligence data, could be found to constitute collusion if accepted by a court. Cory also investigated possible collusion in the car-bomb murders of Lord Justice and Lady Gibson in April 1987 by the Provisional IRA and, in this case, he found no evidence of collusion by the Gardai or any other Government agency.

As Judge Cory explains in the introduction to his reports, his remit while conducting his inquiries was limited: 'The terms of reference pertaining to this inquiry are precise and clear. I have no power to subpoena witnesses or compel the production of documents... My task is to review all the relevant papers pertaining to each case including the records of earlier investigations. In addition, I may interview anyone I think can assist in the examination of the relevant documents.'

Basically, Judge Cory was limited to documented, written evidence, and could not interview potential witnesses or anyone accused. But, as we know, taking the Watergate scandal as a prime example, although conducted by journalists, paper trails can be very revealing (although in that case Nixon's tapes were hugely significant and, of course, Woodward and Bernstein had secretly interviewed witnesses as well).

At the beginning of his Foreword, Judge Cory explained his purpose: 'I was asked by the Government of the United Kingdom to investigate allegations of collusion by members of the security forces in the context of the deaths of Patrick Finucane, Robert Hamill, Rosemary Nelson and Billy Wright and to report recommendations for any further action.' The Cory Collusion Inquiry, and the reports it spawned (running to around 100 pages each on average), were a preliminary probe to see if a full, independent, public and/or judicial inquiry should be held. Public inquiries are enormously expensive and take a long time. It should also be noted that the RUC, the main focus of alleged collusion, had been disbanded three years before Judge Cory's reports were published and made public in 2004.

In the cases of Billy Wright and Robert Hamill, Judge Cory recommended that a full, independent, public inquiry should be held, meaning that he had found evidence which could be found to constitute collusion, if accepted by a court.

The main focus of this book is, of course, Rosemary Nelson. But, as we have seen, the 1989 murder of fellow human rights defence lawyer Pat Finucane has many parallels with Rosemary Nelson's murder. In essence, both Finucane and Nelson represented clients from both sides of the sectarian divide; both of them were highly effective lawyers who were making some headway against alleged human rights abuses against their clients (and themselves and other lawyers) and they both received death threats; both were murdered by Loyalist paramilitaries; both of the murders generated controversial and repeated allegations of State collusion.

The murder of Finucane also hung like a spectre over Rosemary and other Northern Ireland defence lawyers, and Rosemary Nelson and many others repeatedly called for a fully independent, public inquiry into his murder.

In a telephone interview from Canada with Neil Root in September 2010, Judge Peter Cory, now in his mid-eighties, said that his Collusion Inquiry Reports 'had to speak for themselves'. The main findings are provided below in relation to the killings of Pat Finucane and Rosemary Nelson.

THE CORY COLLUSION REPORTS
Patrick Finucane: HC473 Parliamentary Copyright HMSO 2004
Rosemary Nelson: HC473 Parliamentary Copyright HMSO 2004

PATRICK FINUCANE
The main thrust of the allegations of State collusion in the murder of Pat Finucane, gunned down in front of his family on 12 February 1989 (his wife was also injured), are against the Force Research Unit (FRU), the Security Service and RUC Special Branch. The Cory Collusion Report clearly singles out all three organisations for examination.

The FRU is a largely clandestine unit, apparently based at Thiepval Barracks in Northern Ireland. It is essentially a unit whose main function is recruiting and handling agents for undercover assignments and it has a powerful agent-handling capability. It is no secret that the FRU is alleged to have been engaged in collusion with Loyalist paramilitaries and alleged to have contributed to the assassinations of at least 14 Roman Catholics in Northern Ireland between 1987 and 1991, of which the murder of Pat Finucane was one. There is also alleged FRU involvement in the deaths of two senior UDA members, an organisation with close links with Loyalist paramilitaries, which carried out the murder of Pat Finucane.

The allegations of FRU involvement in Finucane's murder is linked to one of its agents, Brian Nelson, who would face trial later. Nelson was an influential figure within the UDA (he acted as the intelligence chief in the organisation), and also an undercover agent being run by the FRU inside the UDA.

The key question about alleged FRU collusion in this case is whether the FRU had 'advance knowledge' that Patrick Finucane was being targeted by the UDA, and the documents accessed 'clearly raise questions', as Judge Cory points out in his report. The judge continued that there seemed to be 'conflicts in the documentary evidence that can only be resolved at a public hearing'.

In 1990, Brian Nelson made a statement (a written record was made) saying that he *had* told his FRU handlers 'about the events leading up to the murder'. Nelson would later retract some evidence that he gave, in 1993, but *not* the fact that he had warned his handlers that the UDA had planned to kill a solicitor (his handlers vehemently denied that he had told them this). Cory states that he is not in a position to reach a conclusion as to whether the FRU had had previous warning of Finucane's targeting before the murder (remembering that Cory only had access to documentary evidence). But Cory does point out six key points that raise valid questions and, as Cory says, 'may lend support to Nelson's assertions' – namely, that he had warned the FRU prior to Finucane's murder on 12 February 1989.

First, on the morning after Finucane's murder, 13 February 1989, Nelson telephoned his FRU handler saying, 'It was ours this morning.' As Cory states, 'From this cryptic comment, the handler was able to divine, with apparent certainty, that Nelson was referring to the murder.' Cory continues that this 'might suggest' that Nelson's handler did have some prior information or knowledge about the targeting of Finucane, and that it had been spoken about before between Nelson and his FRU handler. Second, Nelson was said to have had a conversation with a Loyalist (known in the report as 'Loyalist J') and, in that discussion, Patrick Finucane had been identified as a target. This conversation reportedly took place six to eight weeks before the murder. As Cory makes clear, this was 'the very sort of conversation that was routinely reported by Nelson to his handlers'. So, if this was the kind of intelligence which was being passed by Nelson, is it so difficult to believe that Nelson would have been informed about Finucane's planned assassination, especially as Finucane was a high-profile lawyer?

The next point lends support to the veracity of this conversation between Nelson and Loyalist J. Six days before Finucane's murder, Nelson's FRU handlers knew that Nelson himself was 'initiating most of the targeting for the UDA'. This is an incredible revelation, and shows that Nelson most likely did know about the targeting of Finucane (he was well placed in such matters within the UDA). Cory adds that a Special Branch agent, William Stobie, informed a journalist that Nelson had been present at a meeting where Finucane's targeting was discussed. It should not be forgotten that Nelson was the intelligence chief of the UDA; would the chief of intelligence be unaware of such a major targeting operation? It is very unlikely.

Then the Cory Report informs us that Nelson was under 'considerable pressure' from the UDA at the time, as some UDA operations had gone wrong and he was expected to provide 'reliable targeting information' for the organisation. Could it be alleged that Nelson instigated or was heavily involved in the planning of Finucane's murder himself? Such a target would have earned him kudos within the UDA.

The next point that Cory makes adds to the stress felt by Nelson at the time; he was also under pressure from his FRU handlers, as they had become 'increasingly dissatisfied with his intelligence information'. This meant that Nelson would have been expected to provide his handlers with any intelligence about Finucane's targeting, especially as Cory states that Nelson 'was aware that Patrick Finucane was "a hot target"'.

Cory's final point on whether Nelson informed his FRU handlers about Finucane's targeting before it was carried out is a matter of record. After Finucane's murder, Nelson *did* tell his FRU handlers that he had given photographs of Pat Finucane and another target to Loyalist J. Yet there is no recorded criticism of Nelson about this action by his handlers. Also, as Cory points out, 'if Nelson had, in fact, failed to report the targeting of Finucane in a timely fashion, this would have generated some adverse comment by FRU'. But there was none.

Cory then concluded the section of his report dealing

with whether the FRU knew about Finucane's targeting prior to his murder. Cory wrote that, if what Nelson said was true and he had informed his handlers about the coming murder, and the FRU did nothing 'to either warn Patrick Finucane or otherwise intervene', this 'would be capable of constituting a collusive act'. Cory then calls for a public inquiry, stating that this would be the only way to find out the truth.

But *did* Nelson tell the FRU what he knew prior to the murder? He said that he did, and never wavered from that assertion. Why would Nelson want to lie? Of course, we can make no conclusions here, but let's take a look at Brian Nelson's life, to supply us with all the information possible in the interests of balance, to reach our own judgements about whether Nelson was telling the truth or not.

Brian Nelson was in his early forties at the time of Pat Finucane's murder in 1989. He had been a member of the UDA since the early 1970s after serving in the Black Watch. In 1974, he was convicted of the kidnap and torture of a partially sighted and mentally retarded Catholic, Gerald Higgins (who died soon after), and Nelson was sent to prison for seven years, but served three. After his release, he went to work on construction sites in Germany, that was then enjoying a building boom. But in 1985, he was approached by Military Intelligence and asked to go back to the UDA and go undercover to gain intelligence. Nelson agreed and, over the next few years, he grew in stature within the UDA, becoming responsible for identifying targets and acting as a sort of paramilitary chief intelligence officer. It was in the early Nineties, after Finucane's murder, that

Nelson became the focus of an inquiry led by Sir John Stevens into the murder of a man called Loughlin Maginn. As Judge Cory would do a decade later, Stevens was instructed to investigate possible collusion between the RUC and the paramilitaries. Nelson's fingerprints were discovered on some security documents related to the case, and he was arrested after some legal wrangling.

But, on his arrest, Nelson began to claim that he had been active on behalf of the British Government (through the FRU). The then head of MI5 endorsed Nelson's claim, informing Stevens that Nelson had been working for the British Army and not the RUC (a link between the UDA man Nelson and the RUC would, of course, have constituted collusion in Maginn's murder). However, it was not to be that simple. The RUC had a stronger grip on events in Northern Ireland than the FRU as it operated on the ground day by day. This led to dissension between the RUC and FRU as the depth of Nelson's criminal activities in the UDA while secretly attached to the FRU was exposed.

Brian Nelson then gave a very long statement to the police that took two months to dictate and filled 650 pages. It was in this statement that Nelson made his allegation that he had told the FRU of Finucane's targeting before his murder. He also said in his statement that both the British Army and Loyalist paramilitaries had directed him into making the UDA more effective in assassination operations. To aid him in this goal, he said that the British Army had supplied him with highly confidential documents, including photos and addresses of potential targets, which he then passed on to Loyalist assassins within the UDA. Of course, if this was true, it definitely constitutes an act of purposeful collusion in murder. It also came out that Nelson had supplied targeting intelligence to the UVF, which the FRU had not been able to infiltrate. Nelson said that his intelligence and targeting information became so complex that he had to introduce a 'blue card index system' to organise it. Some paramilitary members never disposed of the blue intelligence cards that Nelson gave them, and the Stevens Inquiry team was able to take Nelson's fingerprints from some of them. In his inquiry report, Sir John Stevens reached the conclusion that Nelson was actually choosing the targets to be assassinated. If this was true, then Nelson must have been very aware of Finucane's targeting, and perhaps had been instrumental in its planning.

However, regarding Nelson's allegation that the FRU had known that Pat Finucane was being lined up to be killed, Stevens did not agree. His report said that Loyalist paramilitaries had approached Nelson for confidential intelligence information about 14 potential Sinn Fein councillors, of whom Finucane was one (Pat Finucane was campaigning to become a councillor). However, Stevens concluded that Nelson gave the information on all 14 to the paramilitaries, but only told the FRU about 10 of the proposed targets. It transpired that the ten who were known to the FRU were never targeted, while the four it did not know about were murdered. Finucane was one of those four, apparently. Stevens said that 'the FRU had been inexcusably careless in failing to protect the four who lost their lives'.

The Stevens Inquiry (not the last to be conducted by him) would come under severe criticism later for not digging deeply enough. When alleged State collusion is being investigated, the conclusion often arrived at is of incompetence, or at worst negligence. Purposeful collusion is very difficult to prove in a court of law and, of course, is a political white-hot potato and, if proven, would be immensely damaging to the reputation of any democratic system.

In 1992, Brian Nelson went on trial. He was accused of not having informed the FRU of all of the paramilitary targeting operations he knew about. Of course, it depends on who you believe – Nelson or the FRU. If what Nelson alleged in his statement was true, it was the FRU itself which gave him the secret intelligence and personal details of key targets to pass on to Loyalist paramilitaries, to facilitate an alleged mutually collusive act to improve the killing capability of the UDA. If this allegation were true, the FRU would almost certainly have known about all 14 targets, including Pat Finucane, before his murder.

At his trial, Brian Nelson repeated that he had warned Military Intelligence of the plans of the UFF (closely connected with the UDA) to kill Finucane, and that this warning had not been passed on to Pat Finucane himself. As part of a guilty plea bargain, Nelson was convicted of twenty charges, including five of conspiracy to murder, but two murder charges were dropped. Brian Nelson got ten years.

After his imprisonment, further allegations began to emerge about his involvement in other murder target operations, some of them high profile. Also, a claim was made by Sinn Fein President Gerry Adams that Nelson had been involved in gun-running from South Africa, comprising large consignments of very serious hardware. Brian Nelson died of a brain haemorrhage on 13 April 2003, aged 55.

So Brian Nelson had been actively employed as an FRU informant in the UDA for several years by the time of Pat Finucane's murder, whether he informed his handlers of Finucane's targeting or not. Nelson was a hardened man, privy to high-level Loyalist paramilitary operations, and undoubtedly a key part in some. It may never be known for sure how much he was involved in Finucane's targeting, however, but, as we have seen, a Special Branch agent reported seeing him present at a paramilitary meeting where that very subject was discussed. Would Nelson have lied about telling the FRU about the plans to murder Pat Finucane? It cannot be ruled out. Nelson was facing a lengthy prison sentence as a result of the Stevens Inquiry, and he may have hit out at his handlers so as to minimise his own culpability, for, if he had informed the FRU, logic dictates that Finucane would have been warned or protected.

However, the evidence supplied by Judge Cory in his report on Finucane shows us that it is equally unlikely that Brian Nelson did not inform his FRU handlers about Finucane's targeting by the UFF/UDA. Nelson was under enormous pressure from both sides – the FRU and the UDA – to provide targeting intelligence. But were the FRU and UDA working towards the same aim, as Nelson insisted? Why would any member of the FRU want Finucane and others dead? Finucane was a Catholic who represented some very high-profile Republican clients, as we have seen. Could the FRU have been working with Loyalist paramilitaries against Republicans, whether through threats, intimidation or the passing of information? As we have recorded, it had been alleged that clients of Rosemary Nelson reported threats to her supposedly from individual officers from the RUC. As Judge Cory points out in his report, only a full and far-reaching, completely public inquiry without agenda or limitations will get to the bottom of that.

The Cory Collusion Report on Pat Finucane's case does go on to focus on two important factors about Brian Nelson and the FRU, and alleged collusion. Firstly, Cory is almost certain that his FRU handlers were passing confidential information to Nelson. Cory gained this from the FRU's own records. Cory states that the records 'leave little doubt that, on occasion, handlers provided information to Nelson that facilitated his targeting activities'. Cory adds that there is 'no indication' that the FRU gave Nelson details about Finucane, but that the fact that information about others was passed 'demonstrates a general pattern of behaviour on the part of Nelson's handlers that could be considered collusive'. Nelson's key role in UDA targeting operations is then mentioned, leading to the conclusion that 'the provision of information to Nelson in these circumstances may be seen as evidence of collusive behaviour that had the potential to facilitate the deadly operations planned by the UDA'.

The second point relates to the fact that the FRU 'were aware, or at the very least, most certainly ought to have been aware, of the criminal acts of Nelson'. It should be remembered that Nelson freely admitted committing criminal acts himself at his trial. Cory is firm in his conclusion here, stating, 'the documents I have examined disclose that army handlers and their superiors turned a blind eye to the criminal acts of Nelson. In doing this they established a pattern of behaviour that could be characterised as collusive.'

Judge Cory's overall conclusion regarding the FRU is that 'the documents either in themselves or taken cumulatively can be taken to indicate that the FRU committed acts of collusion. Further, there is strong if, in some instances, conflicting documentary evidence that the FRU committed collusive acts.' Strong words coming from a former Supreme Court judge.

The next focus of the Cory Report on Finucane is the Security Service, basically MI5 (which is responsible for domestic security within the British Isles), MI6 (SIS – which protects against international threats), and the Joint Security Service (which is an umbrella for both agencies). Cory goes straight in to attack the Security Service, stating that 'the agent operations that the Security Service ran in Northern Ireland did give rise to conduct that appears to fall within the definition of collusion'. This goes back to 1981, when Finucane was very high profile, representing the IRA hunger-strikers including Bobby Sands. Cory points out that the UDA had plans to murder Finucane even in 1981, and that 'the threat was both very real and very imminent'. Security Service officers from the Joint Security Service and SIS and the RUC 'decided to take no steps to intervene or halt the attack'.

Cory also reveals that, in 1985, four years after the 1981 threat and four years before Finucane's murder, the Security Service knew that 'a leading Loyalist paramilitary considered Patrick Finucane to be a priority target'. Also, in December 1988, less than two months before Pat Finucane was murdered, 'the Security Service received information from an agent that there were plans afoot to kill various targets, and that the UDA had singled out Patrick Finucane for special attention'. Cory adds that Pat Finucane was still not warned about the clear and present danger to his life.

The culmination of these facts led Cory to conclude that 'the apparent failure of the Security Service to suggest to RUC Special Branch that action should be taken on these threats, might, itself, be capable of constituting collusive action'.

The final focus in the Cory Collusion Report is RUC Special Branch. There are five aspects of RUC Special Branch conduct outlined in the report, but one of them has been redacted for security reasons. First is the failure of the RUC Special Branch to act on known threats against Finucane, as outlined in the material above regarding the Security Service. In the case of the RUC Special Branch, Cory asserts that 'the protection of agent security was seen as more important than saving the life of a person who faced a serious and imminent threat'. To protect and serve, indeed.

The RUC Special Branch agent William Stobie (who said he saw Brian Nelson present at the meeting planning Finucane's murder) appears again here. It transpires that, only five days before Finucane's murder, 'a top UDA official' approached Stobie, who was asked to supply a 9mm Browning pistol for a hit on a top Provisional IRA man. There is no evidence to suggest that Finucane was a Provisional himself, but he was obviously seen as that in Loyalist circles. Stobie reported this to his bosses, but incredibly 'this information was not apparently pursued'. Then, three days after the Finucane murder, the same UDA man came back to Stobie, asking him to 'pick up and hide a 9mm Browning'. As Cory relays, no effort was made to find and collect this weapon as evidence, 'although there was every reason to believe that it was the firearm used to kill Patrick Finucane'. Cory concludes this point by saying about RUC Special Branch, 'The failure to act on information received in 1989, both before and after the Finucane murder, is indicative of collusion and should be the subject of inquiry at a public hearing.'

Next Cory focuses on the 'Intelligence and Threats books' kept by RUC Special Branch. It is pointed out that RUC Special Branch did not act on intelligence received from FRU. Cory then outlines a sectarian discrepancy in RUC Special Branch conduct at this time. The report states that the RUC Special Branch were passive and 'rarely took any steps to document and prevent attacks by the UDA', but it was proactive in following up information and threats from Republican paramilitaries, including the Provisional IRA. Cory stipulates that this failure of the RUC Special Branch 'often led to tragic consequences' and that it 'constitutes a pattern of conduct that could be equated with collusive behaviour'.

Cory's final point about RUC Special Branch is that it withheld information from the Detective Superintendent (name redacted) investigating Pat Finucane's murder. This was ostensibly information about the role of Brian Nelson in the FRU and the role of William Stobie in RUC Special Branch. Cory asserts that this withholding of information 'did much to frustrate the investigation'. It is added that RUC Special Branch 'knew, or certainly ought to have known' that this was key information needed to carry out a full investigation into Pat Finucane's murder.

Judge Peter Cory was firm in his conclusion to his Collusion Report on Patrick Finucane. Referring to all the documents he had looked at and the facts he had gleaned from them, he concluded: 'There is strong evidence that collusive acts were committed by the Army (FRU), the RUC Special Branch and the Security Service. I am satisfied that there is a need for a public inquiry.'

ROSEMARY NELSON

The Cory Collusion Report into Rosemary Nelson's murder is divided into two parts. The first covers threats and alleged threats made against her, as well as an examination of the knowledge Government agencies had of these threats. The threats and alleged threats against Rosemary Nelson have been covered in detail earlier in this book, so will not be repeated here. Judge Cory's conclusions, however, about the amount that Government agencies knew of these threats and whether their actions or non-actions could constitute collusion bear further examination.

The second part of the Cory Report focuses on the investigation of the unusually active security activity on the weekend before her murder as well as the investigation of the people suspected of carrying it out, both of which are explored here.

Judge Cory's introduction has subtitles of 'The Failure to Protect Rosemary Nelson' and 'Background to This Murder'. In the latter subsection, Cory draws attention to the parallels with the murder of Pat Finucane, almost exactly a decade all but a month earlier. Cory outlines the threat posed to defence lawyers by paramilitaries in Northern Ireland, and states that, at the time of Finucane's murder, the British Government had known that 'two other defence solicitors had also been explicitly targeted by paramilitaries'. There is then reference made to the UN Special Rapporteur's Report on the Independence of Judges and Lawyers in Northern Ireland, and that Finucane's murder was still casting a dark shadow of fear over the legal community a decade later. Some defence lawyers had been changing their working practices or giving up criminal law entirely. The alleged threats made by the RUC towards Rosemary Nelson and many other defence lawyers is then mentioned, followed by a section explaining why judges and lawyers need to be respected in the interests of the upholding of justice and those who deliver it.

The conduct of the State (the British Government and the agencies that operate in its name) is, of course, the key focus of the Cory Report. The conduct of the RUC and the NIO before and after the murder are examined in regard to alleged State collusion. As already stated, the threats and alleged threats against Rosemary Nelson, and the Government knowledge and response to them, have been covered earlier, so Judge Cory's conclusions will suffice here.

First, Judge Cory looks at the behaviour of the RUC. Regarding the alleged threats and derogatory comments made about Rosemary Nelson to her clients by RUC officers, the conclusion is clear. Cory states, 'If they are found to have been made, [they] are capable of constituting collusion, both as evidence of turning a blind eye to all threats made to her and as encouraging others to attack her.'

Next, there is the alleged 'verbal and physical abuse' directed at Rosemary Nelson at Garvaghy Road when she introduced herself as the lawyer of the GRRC to RUC officers. Cory found that, if the allegations were true, 'they, too, could constitute evidence of collusion, both as to the turning a blind eye to threats to her and as encouraging others to abuse and threaten her'.

Next is whether the RUC failed to properly investigate the complaints of alleged threatening remarks from RUC officers. Cory concludes that, if it were found to be true, 'that could constitute evidence of collusion both by turning a blind eye to threats to her and by encouraging threats by others or by indicating that they would be tolerated'. Also, it was alleged that Sir Ronnie Flanagan, the Chief Constable of the RUC, had told the UN Special Rapporteur in an interview (as Mr Cumaraswamy insisted he did) that solicitors were working for paramilitaries. Cory asserts that, if this were found to be true, that 'could constitute evidence of collusion by encouraging others to think of solicitors as being paramilitary members or terrorists who could be treated as such'.

Then the Cory Report looks at how the RUC dealt with the threats facing Rosemary Nelson, setting the alleged threats that the RUC itself had made against her aside for the moment. Cory cites five instances where the RUC's response to threats to Rosemary Nelson before her murder 'could constitute evidence that it was turning a blind eye' to the threat it contained. The threats themselves have been outlined earlier in this book. These are: (i) the RUC's failure to respond to the pamphlet *The Man Without a Future*; (ii) the failure to follow up on the 3 June death-threat letter; (iii) the repeated 'failure to become aware' of the same letter by the RUC when it resurfaced in the Mulvihill Inquiry; (iv) the overall failure of the RUC to take measures to protect solicitors such as Rosemary taking on high-profile Nationalist cases despite Pat Finucane's murder; and (v) the failure of the RUC to 'attach any weight' to letters sent to them from reputable organisations concerned about Nelson's safety. The latter point asserts that this 'turning of a blind eye' could also constitute collusion.

Next, the report looks at the role of the NIO in dealing with the threats against Rosemary Nelson before her murder. The NIO came in for criticism in six instances, the five above and one other: 'The NIO failed to offer Rosemary Nelson protection under its own protection scheme although it was aware or should have been aware of the dangers to her. This, too, could be found to be turning a blind eye.'

The next deals with two points focusing on the conduct of the RUC and NIO after Rosemary's murder. The first is that the RUC and NIO denied that they knew of 'any specific threat' to Rosemary Nelson, although 'both were aware or should have been aware' of the threats outlined above, plus alleged threatening incidents. The second point is that the NIO 'were prepared to take the position' that they had no record of a request for protection made on behalf of Rosemary Nelson by her clients the GRRC. However, 'it knew or ought to have known' that a request had been made at a meeting.

Summing up this section of the report, Cory states,

'Although these actions after the murder cannot standing alone constitute collusive acts, they may be seen as a part of a cumulative pattern of conduct which could be found to be collusive.'

Regarding the investigation into Rosemary Nelson's murder, eventually led by Colin Port, the Deputy Chief Constable of Norfolk, Cory states that, despite difficulties, 'The investigation carried out by the Port inquiry team was, in every way, exemplary.'

On the subject of the enhanced security presence in the vicinity of the Nelson home on the weekend before her murder, Cory states that, on the basis of the evidence he had seen, 'I am satisfied that the increased security force activity is not evidence of collusive activity.' He added that this activity did not aid Rosemary's murder, or turn a blind eye to the planting of the bomb under her car.

Before outlining his strict guidelines of transparency and thoroughness regarding public inquiries, Judge Cory concludes his report by saying that 'there must be a public inquiry regarding the failure of the RUC and NIO to provide some form of protection for Rosemary Nelson'.

In summary, the Cory Collusion Inquiry Reports published in 2004 recommended that, in the cases of Patrick Finucane, Robert Hamill, Billy Wright and Rosemary Nelson, full public inquiries should be carried out to investigate allegations of British security force and State collusion in their murders.

In the case of Patrick Finucane, no public inquiry has been conducted, more than 20 years after his murder and 7 years after Cory's recommendation. This is largely due to the fact that the Security Service is allegedly suppressing key documents that would not allow a thorough investigation. In April 2005, Pat Finucane's widow Geraldine wrote to all the senior judges in Britain asking them not to sit on any proposed Patrick Finucane inquiry as it stood. However, the Finucane family, the Pat Finucane Centre and other prominent people and organisations continue to lobby for a full, thorough and open independent, public inquiry, which is the least that they deserve.

Regarding the murder of Robert Hamill, the preliminary hearing of the Robert Hamill Inquiry opened on 24 May 2005 in Portadown, but did not start its full hearing until January 2009. The results have yet to be released.

The results of the Billy Wright Inquiry were released in September 2010, as detailed earlier in this book and showed negligence, not collusion.

The Rosemary Nelson Inquiry opened at the Craigavon Civic Centre in April 2005, but the full hearings did not start until 2008. The next chapter deals with those hearings in detail.

On 7 June 2005, before any of the full hearings were under way, the British Government, under the aegis of then Prime Minister Tony Blair, passed the Inquiries Act 2005. This limited the scope of public inquiries, and would directly affect the inquiries proposed by Cory the year before. It replaced the Tribunals of Inquiry (Evidence) Act 1921, which had allowed the chairman of a public inquiry complete freedom.

Judge Cory has criticised the passing of this Act and told the US Congressional Hearings into Human Rights in Northern Ireland in March 2005 (before the Act was passed) that it would make 'a meaningful inquiry impossible'. Judge Cory told Congress, 'The minister, the actions of whose ministry was to be reviewed by the public inquiry, would have the authority to thwart the efforts of the inquiry at every step. It really creates an intolerable *Alice in Wonderland* situation.'

9

THE ROSEMARY NELSON INQUIRY

The Rosemary Nelson Inquiry (RNI) held its opening preliminary hearing in April 2005 at the Craigavon Civic Centre, Craigavon, County Armagh. However, it would be another three years before it held its first full day of hearings. In September 2006, MI5, Britain's domestic Security Service, was granted permission to take part in the RNI. This was a significant development, as permission to participate fully had only previously been given to the Nelson family, the NIO, the Ministry of Defence (MoD) and Colin Port, the leader of the murder investigation. Rosemary Nelson's family immediately criticised this move, as they felt that MI5 could possibly remove or redact classified information which they could state was a threat to security, a real consideration in the dangerous and complex political landscape of Northern Ireland. But the real concern was that key information that could get to the truth about who was culpable for the murder of Rosemary Nelson could be removed from evidence. Rosemary Nelson's brother Eunan voiced this concern. The main worry was that any evidence pointing to alleged State collusion in her murder could disappear, making it much more difficult to arrive at – or even approach – justice.

Reaction was also swift from prominent politicians. Dolores Kelly, a member of the SDLP Policing Board, told *The News Letter*, a Belfast publication, on 22 September 2006, 'Why would MI5 want to be involved in the Nelson inquiry? Is it because they had intelligence about Rosemary's murder? If so, what did they do with it?' She went on to raise her concern that this could mean that MI5 intended to take a more active role in Northern Ireland policing in the future.

The former MI5 agent and whistleblower Annie Machon was approached by the authors, but she said that she could be of little assistance, as she had left MI5 several years before Rosemary Nelson's murder.

The Sinn Fein Upper Bann Assembly member John O'Dowd was direct, saying, 'There is a widely held belief that British State agents were directly involved in her murder. This belief has been strengthened over the years as successive RUC and PSNI regimes have sought to frustrate and delay the search for the truth.'

There was a Procedural Hearing in October 2007 to outline how the RNI would proceed. The first day of full hearings was on Tuesday, 15 April 2009 under the chairmanship of Sir Michael Morland, a retired High Court judge. The inquiry had already taken more than 250 statements, but this was the first day of open hearings. It was more than nine years after her murder, and almost seven years since the RUC had been stood down to be replaced by the PSNI (although most members of the RUC had joined the new police force, and many saw it as a rebranding). There was a wide array of Counsel and Instructing Solicitors representing key participants at the inquiry hearings. Different Queen's Counsel (QC) and solicitors represented the inquiry itself, with other participants including Rosemary Nelson's widower Paul and their children, as well as her mother Sheila, the PSNI, Colin Port and his investigation team, the NIO, the MoD and the Security Service MI5.

Rosemary Nelson's brother Eunan said as the inquiry opened that it was 'something that we have to do in order to be able to move on with our own lives'.

The RNI would run for 130 days, before it retired to consider the complex evidence received. This chapter attempts to extract the key and relevant evidence given, to present a clearer picture of what is known or alleged. The evidence is complex and lengthy, but also enlightening and sometimes shocking. For those readers who want a comprehensive look at the hearings, please refer to the RNI and BIRW websites (http://www.rosemarynelsoninquiry.org/ and http://www.birw.org/).]

THE HEARINGS

Leading Counsel for the Inquiry, Rory Phillips QC, opened the first day of hearings of the inquiry on 15 April 2008. He started by outlining the facts of Rosemary Nelson's murder, and gave an overview of the circumstances that led to it. These included her work as a defence lawyer representing controversial clients, allegations of State collusion, the death threats she received and the turbulent political climate in Northern Ireland in March 1999. He then pointed out that the inquiry was going ahead under the directive of Section 44 of the Police (Northern Ireland) Act 1998, and not the recently passed Inquiries Act 2005. As we have seen, the latter had attracted much criticism, including from Judge Peter Cory, and so the fact that it was not directing the RNI was a relief to many.

Rory Phillips QC then summarised the three main focus areas of the RNI: (i) an examination of questions about the lead-up to Rosemary Nelson's murder; (ii) an analysis of questions about the investigation of her murder; (iii) recommendations (conclusions from evidence heard and gathered). He then stipulated that the phrase 'other State agency' which would be heard throughout the hearings would include MI5.

Next, he stated that the question of those suspected of Rosemary's murder (nobody had been convicted) would also be included, as it was integral to the examination of whether there had been any 'wrongful act or omission' which had allowed her murder to happen. This was obviously referring to alleged State collusion or negligence, through the vessel of the security forces in Northern Ireland. But he went on to say that the inquiry was not a criminal trial and any findings would not result in criminal liability. Phillips then assured those present that the Attorney General had promised that no criminal prosecution would be taken against anyone giving evidence (unless they perjured themselves), in the interests of open and honest testimony.

Phillips admitted that there were some gaps in the inquiry's documentary record, and that some witnesses had expressed concern that there were documents that had not been disclosed to the inquiry. However, he said that all State parties had given statements showing how they had made efforts to follow disclosure guidelines. He then focused on evidence from computer and paper files, saying that the inquiry had had direct access to them, and that the PSNI had given the inquiry a brief outline document of their computer systems. But when a more detailed outline was asked for, specifically looking at who had direct control of these databases, no statement or larger outline had been forthcoming, nor any reason given why not.

Phillips then said that the PSNI had been asked whether RUC Special Branch had ever held any paper intelligence file on Rosemary Nelson, and that the PSNI had said that 'no personal file paper existed on Rosemary Nelson prior to her murder'. In March 2008, Colin Port, the leader of the murder investigation had confirmed this. However, this would prove controversial later, and Phillips said that he expected some witnesses to be questioned about this during the hearings. He added that 254 statements out of 341 given would be used by the inquiry, and, out of those 254, 115 witnesses would give evidence during the hearings.

The matter of witness anonymity was then highlighted, as well as the redaction policy (the omission of names or security-sensitive facts). Phillips said that there had been applications from 144 witnesses for anonymity (a high number, but not surprising), and decisions had been made in 110 of those cases, and the others would follow as the hearings progressed. In the case of ciphered intelligence (largely used by security forces), the ciphers would remain in place until the anonymity request of the witness was decided, or if challenged.

Phillips then spoke about the focus of the second part of the inquiry. This included how much Rosemary Nelson had interested the intelligence agencies and the consequent effect on the attitudes of the State agencies and security forces. It would also include whether security intelligence on Rosemary had been known outside of Government departments and intelligence agencies and, if so, if this had affected her personal safety and security. To get to the bottom of this, he said that the inquiry would have to examine how the intelligence agencies worked in Northern Ireland in the late 1990s. For this purpose, statements had been taken from those in the intelligence community at that time at all levels within the PSNI, the Security Service MI5 and the British Army, and some would probably be called to the hearings.

Phillips then addressed the third part of the inquiry's focus. This was to do with security force actions, what occurred at the scene of Rosemary Nelson's murder and the question of obstruction. On the latter point, he said that the inquiry was still waiting for key statements and documents needed to examine the question of obstruction.

Finally, Phillips spoke about the first focus of the inquiry: the lead-up to Rosemary Nelson's murder. This would include files concerning Rosemary's safety and allegations and threats made against her, the complaints made by her and on her behalf, and the controversial events around Drumcree and the Garvaghy Road, in which Rosemary Nelson was of course central.

Phillips ended the first day of hearings by giving an

overview of the political situation in Northern Ireland in the lead-up to Rosemary Nelson's murder, to put it in context.

The second day of hearings began with Rory Phillips QC continuing his political overview of Northern Ireland in the 1990s. He then focused on the Drumcree marches, showing a map of the annual disputed parades, and saying how important they were to the RNI as the conflicts in Drumcree in 1996 and 1997 had ramped up tensions and animosity between Loyalists and Republicans in Northern Ireland. Other causes of increased tension he cited were the 1997 Portadown murder of Robert Hamill and the murder of two RUC officers in Lurgan.

He then turned to the subject of policing in Northern Ireland, highlighting the powers brought in by the Prevention of Terrorism Act and the Emergency Powers Act, which had changed the whole complexion of policing. He added that the police (then the RUC) had obviously felt they needed these powers but, as a result, the RUC had become an anti-terrorist organisation instead of a community police force. With the background now complete, Phillips then addressed specific issues.

He then played four video film clips of Rosemary Nelson. The first showed her in June 1997 after the arrest of her client Colin Duffy, accused of murdering the two RUC officers in Lurgan. The second showed Rosemary talking about the assault she had alleged had been made on her by RUC officers on the Garvaghy Road in July 1997. Phillips pointed out that this was the foundation of a legal action that Rosemary Nelson had started against the Chief Constable of the RUC, Sir Ronnie Flanagan, shortly before her murder. Phillips also said that one of the complaints made by Rosemary over the alleged assault was that the identification numbers of the RUC officers had been covered up so that she could not make a complaint against them personally. The next video showed an interview with Rosemary talking about her views of the political situation in Northern Ireland, at the end of which she was asked about her role as a lawyer in Northern Ireland. She replied that that was 'a contradiction in terms', plainly meaning 'lawyer' and 'Northern Ireland'.

The fourth film clip was a recording of Rosemary giving evidence before the US Congressional Committee. In it she described the alleged threats made by police officers to her clients, the confusion in her role as a Northern Ireland defence lawyer and the association of her name with paramilitary activity. Phillips told the RNI hearings that on this occasion Rosemary had also made a connection between herself and Pat Finucane, regarding the threats made against her and the dangers she faced.

He then said that the inquiry would look into Rosemary's work and legal practice, and what about it had caused conflict with others, adding that a wide range of her staff between 1989 and 1999 had made statements as evidence. Phillips then gave an outline of Rosemary's legal career, and made the suggestion that her work with her clients Colin Duffy and the GRRC had done the most to bring her into the political sphere.

Phillips then touched on a controversial point. He spoke about the rumours doing the rounds that Rosemary's relationship with her client Colin Duffy had been more than just a professional one, and that she had allegedly had an affair with him. He added that these rumours might have affected how Rosemary was viewed, although those who believed the grapevine (or a tiny minority of them) would not have wanted her murdered because of it alone. Neil Root contacted Colin Duffy in prison in August 2010, and this was one of the questions he put to him. There was no reply.

Phillips stated that the paramilitary murders that Colin Duffy had been accused of were very high profile and controversial, and that Rosemary Nelson's vocal work on his behalf had helped make her much more widely known and high profile herself, therefore making her more vulnerable. He then went on to the subject of the treatment of lawyers in Northern Ireland and that many human rights organisations and charities had expressed their concerns in writing. He also said that the inquiry had received statements from practising lawyers stating their concerns about their treatment and emergency legislation which had changed key professional areas. These included the subject of client access to lawyers and the way interviews had been conducted, including comments made to their clients, which, of course, Rosemary had also alleged. The day's hearings concluded with a summary of the history of the alleged intimidation of defence lawyers in Northern Ireland, and that these problems had begun to be recognised on an international level, especially with Rosemary Nelson and the UN Special Rapporteur.

The following day was taken up with 'complaints procedure' and the framework by which it operated. He said that the complaints process used by the RUC had been changed in 1988, and that the ICPC had been founded in 1987, as a body to oversee the investigation of complaints, which they did in about 70 per cent of cases. The 1998 complaints made by Rosemary Nelson were very significant, as, for the first time in a decade, the ICPC had said that it was not satisfied with the RUC investigation of her complaints. Phillips then spoke about 'G Department' of the RUC, which had dealt with complaints, and its head had been the Deputy Chief Constable of the RUC, with day-to-day charge taken by an Assistant Chief Constable. G Department had dealt with around 2,000–3,000 complaints every year, although, as some complaint investigations took a long time, in some years there were 4,000 being dealt with. In 1997, the Hayes Report, which had examined the police complaints framework and procedure, had found some areas to be unsatisfactory.

Focusing on Rosemary Nelson, Phillips said that she had made around 115 complaints on behalf of her clients between 1996 and 1999, although the inquiry had examined the files and found that there had been around 230 complaints from her legal practice in the same period in total. However, he added that this volume of complaints was not 'remarkable'. Some complaints were always dropped, but, of those that went through, a very large majority was found to be unsubstantiated after G Department investigation. The key complaints made by Rosemary Nelson for the inquiry were three that had been looked at by Commander Mulvihill in his report, those varied ones made against RUC officers, two involving soldiers, and the alleged assault on the Garvaghy Road in 1997.

Starting with the so-called 'Mulvihill complaints', it was explained that these comprised one from the Lawyers Alliance for Justice in Ireland (LAJI) about alleged death threats to Rosemary made by an RUC officer at Gough Barracks. Then there were those from Rosemary Nelson and Colin Duffy over his June 1997 arrest. There was also a June 1998 complaint from Castlereagh by Rosemary Nelson and a ciphered client (name coded). Phillips said that one of these complaints was a threat to Rosemary's life, while the others were regarding negative and insulting comments, including alleged suggestions of Rosemary's association with the Provisional IRA.

Complaints remained under the spotlight into the fifth day of hearings, when Phillips said that the ICPC had pointed out a new form of 'unusual' complaint against the RUC. But he said that this could still have been investigated under the RUC complaint framework, and that this would have left the RUC Chief Constable in charge of the complaints investigation. He also added that it might have been possible to do everything internally, without the ICPC's concerns becoming public. The Secretary of State for Northern Ireland, Mo Mowlam, had written to Sir Ronnie Flanagan, the RUC Chief Constable, stating that she felt the subject was of political importance. She suggested some 'defensive lines' in that letter, answers to tricky questions that could come up if the matter went public, so that all State agencies would have a uniform response. Basically, it was an exercise in public relations damage limitation. Phillips pointed out that this was not ordinary procedure, thus making these complaints different. The NIO also prepared statements in case of public disclosure. But in the end, the ICPC report was not issued to the public.

Phillips then moved on to Commander Mulvihill's investigation into the complaints. Mulvihill had interviewed four clients of Rosemary's who had made complaints. One of them was a client who was arrested on a public-disorder offence, concerning the use of blast bombs on the Garvaghy Road on 29 June 1998. This client had complained that an RUC officer at Castlereagh Barracks had allegedly told him that 'uniformed officers would only see what they wanted to see'. An RUC officer also allegedly referred to Rosemary Nelson as 'a Provi', meaning that she was a member of the Provisional IRA. However, as we saw earlier in this book, in January 1999, two months before Rosemary's murder, Mulvihill had concluded that no criminal proceedings should be carried out against the RUC officers accused. As Phillips would state later in that day's hearing, the ICPC had accepted that these allegations were unproven on 4 November 1998.

On the next day of hearings, Phillips continued his description of the complaints made by Rosemary Nelson and her clients. First, he spoke about a complaint made by Brian Loughran on 26 January 1998. It concerned comments allegedly made about Rosemary Nelson by RUC officers when he was arrested. However, he had given no details of what they had allegedly said, and his complaint was not upheld after it was investigated, and the ICPC had agreed with this verdict. Second, Phillips spoke about a complaint made by Shane McCrory, who had been arrested on 15 December 1997. The scene of this complaint was the back of a police car, when an RUC officer had allegedly told McCrory that Rosemary Nelson 'won't be here that long, she will be dead'. The RUC had filed this complaint as 'incivility', but, as Phillips said, this complaint was more serious than that. Rosemary had been informed and the RUC investigation officer had made 'considerable attempts' to interview Rosemary, but she had not co-operated. The accused officers were interviewed, and they denied the allegations. There was no further action taken, and it was decided that the interviews had been properly conducted.

The next complaint concerned a client who had been detained at Castlereagh Barracks from 21 to 27 February 1998, concerning a murder allegedly carried out by the IRA. Rosemary Nelson had had consultations with him during this time. The RUC officers interviewing him allegedly made 'derogatory comments' about Rosemary, and so she asked to be present at the rest of the interviews. However, the RUC relocated her client, and so they 'noted' that her request was no longer applicable. The matter was taken up by the ICPC, and a BIRW executive prepared a dossier on the case, which Phillips made reference to at the hearings that day. The client had claimed that RUC officers had allegedly called Rosemary 'half-face' (referring to her facial disfigurement), and that 'we have been doing this for 30 years and she won't be able to stop us', as outlined earlier in this book.

At the time of the client's detention, the talks that would lead to the Good Friday Agreement were going on. Rosemary Nelson told an Irish Government civil servant on 3 March 1998 that RUC officers had allegedly told her client that he was being detained 'to keep Sinn Fein permanently excluded from the talks'. Rosemary also claimed that RUC officers had also told her client that 'Rosemary Nelson works for the IRA and takes her orders from them'. Rosemary also told the civil servant that similar statements had been made to other clients, and that the RUC Chief Constable Sir Ronnie Flanagan believed that she was working for paramilitaries, too, as part of their political campaign.

Phillips then outlined the letter sent by Paul Mageean of the CAJ to the British Security Minister Adam Ingram. In the letter, details were given of a client of Rosemary Nelson's who had alleged that RUC officers had told him that he would be 'set up by the LVF' (who, as we know, were behind Rosemary Nelson's murder). Also, the client alleged, remarks were made about Rosemary to the effect that the IRA were 'pulling her strings' and 'there was a new law passed in 1989 which meant they could do away with solicitors who concocted stories'.

Phillips then referred to a letter from Jane Winter of BIRW to Mo Mowlam on 19 March 1998. In the letter, Jane Winter said that Sir Ronnie Flanagan's 'insensitivity to the problem is undoubtedly responsible for the fact that RUC officers on the ground continue to abuse Rosemary Nelson'. An investigation into this particular complaint took place and the RUC officers in question were interviewed. An RUC officer gave a detailed statement that included his belief that 'this is a concerted effort not by the person making the complaint, but by the solicitors to attempt to show system in complaints made against me and then by blackening my character'.

Phillips went back to the subject of the CAJ's letter to the Security Minister Adam Ingram, referring to the 7 July 1998 response from Mr Ingram's private secretary. It said:

'I have to say that the Government is not aware of evidence of... a pattern of police harassment of defence lawyers.' Phillips told the hearing that this was a surprising statement, due to the volume of evidence that the inquiry had examined to the contrary, and that Mr Ingram might be interviewed by the inquiry on this subject.

Phillips then stated that it was not just complaints that were being examined by the inquiry, but also the larger question of just who was aware of the threats to Rosemary Nelson's life. He added that the complaints were also helpful in finding out who knew what, and that these complaints were not tainted by the fact that the complainants could expect financial compensation by making them. He then explained how some people made police complaints as a prelude to taking out a civil action with the hope of compensation. He stipulated that this was not true in this case.

Phillips said that the inquiry faced a 'black-and-white situation'. This, he said, was a choice between two views: that the RUC had behaved disgracefully towards Rosemary Nelson and her fellow defence lawyers; or that Rosemary Nelson was a front for the IRA.

He put this in context by saying that 'these battles were taking place along old and familiar lines', all of which have been outlined earlier in this book. The rest of that day's hearing was taken up by complaints made by Rosemary Nelson and her clients, also examined earlier.

The next day's focus was the alleged physical assault by RUC officers on Rosemary Nelson on the Garvaghy Road. This incident was the thrust of Rosemary's legal action taken against the RUC Chief Constable in January 1999. The RUC investigation had concluded that, although there were multiple allegations of 'incivility' by the RUC towards Rosemary, only one civilian witness, Tom Cusack, had seen the assault take place. There was no medical evidence, the video evidence was inconclusive, and the police officers could not be identified (although we know that Rosemary Nelson claimed that their ID numbers had been obscured). The RUC Chief Inspector in charge of this investigation reached the conclusion that there was insufficient evidence to prosecute any individual RUC officer. The ICPC had pronounced itself satisfied with this conclusion on 30 October 2000, and the DPP had confirmed that no prosecution would take place on 19 January 2001.

Phillips then focused on the intervention of the UN Special Rapporteur and organisations such as Amnesty International, in calling for an investigation into the threats against Rosemary prior to her murder. Towards the end of that day's hearing, a senior civil servant's statement was read out by Phillips, in which the civil servant said that, although threat assessments had found her not to be at risk, 'However, we were worried about Rosemary Nelson's security. On the other hand... we were not prepared to break the KPPS [Key Persons Protection Scheme] and risk opening the floodgates.'

At the end of that day, Phillips focused on the response to the UN Special Rapporteur Param Cumaraswamy's report. An NIO memo from 12 February 1998 was read out that said that 'little of the report is positive'. The key focus was on Cumaraswamy's criticism of 'a suggestion by the [RUC] Chief Constable that solicitors may be working for paramilitaries'. Phillips interpreted this as

Cumaraswamy saying that the RUC had repeatedly claimed to him that solicitors were working for paramilitaries, but that he had never been given any evidence of this. The UN Special Rapporteur was also concerned that solicitors were being identified with the causes of their clients. Cumaraswamy was 'satisfied that there has been harassment and intimidation of defence lawyers by RUC officers'.

On Day 10 of the hearings, Rory Phillips QC started the day's business by looking at a November 1999 BIRW report. This dealt with the response by the British Government to threats against the GRRC. As shown earlier, Tony Blair's Chief of Staff Jonathan Powell had said at a meeting on 18 July 1998 that the security of the GRRC was the subject of concern, and action needed to be urgently taken. Three days later, Powell stated that he would order the NIO to 'attend to the security of the GRRC within the next 48 hours'. Although Rosemary Nelson was not comfortable with the fact that a security assessment was being made by the RUC, as she held the belief that the RUC was the main source of threats against her, she sanctioned the GRRC to apply to the NIO-run KPPS on her behalf. However, Phillips highlighted the fact that Paul Mageean of the CAJ stated that Rosemary felt that the KPPS was not a viable option.

The hearing heard how the GRRC had made repeated efforts to get protection for Rosemary Nelson and for itself, although it was still a subject of debate whether Rosemary was ever singled out personally in these efforts. An official of the NIO spoke to Breandan Mac Cionnaith, a senior member of the GRRC, on 23 July 2008 regarding security worries. The same NIO official had written an internal memo stating that he had told Mac Cionnaith that KPPS applications had to be made by individuals, and that decisions would be taken on the advice of the RUC Chief Constable Sir Ronnie Flanagan. Mac Cionnaith had asked for admission to the KPPS for himself, a councillor and other coalition partners. Mac Cionnaith had outlined the threats made against him, in the form of anonymous phone calls, and how two people had gone into a community centre in his absence looking for him. Somebody in the community centre had identified one of those people (from a newspaper photo) of being a close associate of then LVF leader Billy Wright. Phillips added that Mac Cionnaith had not faxed details of these threats as a follow-up to the NIO official. Rosemary Nelson, lawyer for the GRRC, had also requested 'personal protection weapons' for Mac Cionnaith and a councillor. However, the NIO official had left the KPPS department of the NIO the day after the meeting with Mac Cionnaith, and had written a letter to RUC Special Branch, asking it to carry out a threat analysis on Mac Cionnaith and the councillor.

On the day of Rosemary Nelson's murder, 15 March 1999, Mac Cionnaith immediately issued a press release. It stated: 'The British Government also bear a heavy responsibility at the very highest levels for Rosemary's murder. During talks between representatives of Portadown's Nationalist community and Jonathan Powell... and on a number of occasions since... [the GRRC] has asked that Rosemary Nelson be provided proper protection under the [KPPS]. The British Government refused every request.' But Phillips pointed out that no protection request focused on Rosemary

Nelson had been made at the 23 July meeting between Mac Cionnaith and the NIO official.

This was, of course, all tied up with the controversial parades through Drumcree, and more meetings had taken place, between the GRRC, the Orange Order (Loyalists) and NIO negotiators. Phillips then made reference to a 26 August 1998 letter from Mac Cionnaith to one of the NIO representatives. Mac Cionnaith had written that 'the attitude of authorities and the RUC in particular to the ongoing intimidation of Catholic families... reinforces the view [of]... complete lack of commitment to protect the rights of Portadown Nationalists at all times'. Phillips told the hearing that this was in no way about personal security.

Continuing on the RUC response to these threats, Phillips referred to a letter dated 31 August 1998 from RUC Special Branch to the NIO KPPS department. It said that RUC Special Branch had concluded that it had no evidence of a specific threat against Councillor Mac Cionnaith and a fellow councillor, and that their threat level would remain at Level 4, one level below the level required for KPPS inclusion. With reference to an internal NIO memo dated 3 September, Phillips told the hearing that the NIO official had written that a Level 4 threat assessment would have finished the application, but that she knew that there was 'a political dimension' to this particular case.

The NIO official did follow up, writing to RUC Special Branch to ask if the threat level had changed due to the parades and the Omagh bombing the month before, and also attached a copy of the *Man Without a Future* leaflet. As we know, this made attacks on both MacCionnaith and his lawyer Rosemary Nelson. RUC Special Branch wrote back on 13 September, saying that the Level 4 assessment stood, and that Sir Ronnie Flanagan had said that, although Mac Cionnaith would be at 'considerable risk' in a Loyalist area, this was also a fact for many people.

The final advice was given to Mo Mowlam on 26 October 1998, and it said that Mac Cionnaith saw the admittance of himself and his fellow councillor to the KPPS as an opportunity for the British Government to show good faith, especially as talks were then ongoing. Mowlam responded on 27 October, saying that she did not wish to go against RUC advice. One of the NIO negotiators involved in talks with the GRRC then verbally told Mowlam that this was the wrong decision. The decision was changed soon after, and there was a suggestion that Tony Blair had personally got involved and asked Mowlam to reconsider.

Following this acceptance to the KPPS, an NIO official met Mac Cionnaith in Lurgan to talk about security measures to be taken. The official later said that Mac Cionnaith had asked if protection could be approved for other unnamed GRRC members, and that there had been no mention of Rosemary Nelson. It was alleged also by another official that the GRRC position was that it would not participate in talks until it had protection for all its members, but this was almost impossible, as the acceptance of just Mac Cionnaith and his fellow councillor to the KPPS had been difficult enough. Phillips made reference to several NIO internal memos which showed the view that the NIO thought that Mac Cionnaith was hiding behind the personal protection question to delay making any concessions in talks.

The viability of GRRC personal protection being funded by a charitable trust was then raised, and a meeting took place to look at that. At the meeting, Mac Cionnaith said that Rosemary Nelson had been on the end of 'constant harassment from the RUC' and that she wanted to make a request for protection, but did not want to endure the application process alone. Later, when the GRRC put forward protection funding figures, the charitable trust said that it could not possibly afford the amounts laid out, giving the GRRC the chance to submit revised figures, but this was not done.

Phillips then said that at this time Rosemary Nelson was in no way under consideration for the KPPS, but smaller security actions were being looked into, possibly involving the charitable trust. Phillips then told the hearing that the question was whether Rosemary Nelson had ever specifically been put forward for the KPPS or not, as the thrust of the BIRW report depended on this. Phillips then referred to a statement that said that most people on the street would have considered Rosemary Nelson in need of protection.

Rosemary Nelson was herself present at a meeting between the Prime Minister Tony Blair and the GRRC on 18 January 1999, less than two months before her murder. Phillips told the inquiry hearing that there was no record of Rosemary Nelson's personal security being raised at this meeting. The leader of the UUP, David Trimble, told the Prime Minister that 'extremists from the Red Hand Defenders were increasing the level of violence and one day someone would get killed'. The Red Hand Defenders were of course the LVF-front group that claimed responsibility for Rosemary's murder. The fact that

Trimble had told Tony Blair this was recorded in a memo from 10 Downing Street to the NIO dated 11 March 1999, just four days before Rosemary Nelson's murder.

Tony Blair and the GRRC met again a fortnight after the murder, on 30 March 1999. Briefing papers from that meeting made it clear that 'we have no record of Rosemary Nelson's security being raised with Jonathan Powell', as Phillips told the hearing. He added that Mac Cionnaith had not yet given a statement to the inquiry, and that his evidence could be very interesting to it. Phillips then began to sum up the day's evidence.

He said that the NIO-run KPPS had shown some flexibility, and that Rosemary Nelson had not been 'a leading light of the Coalition [GRRC] itself', but a legal adviser to it. He added that the minutes of the various meetings that Rosemary attended did not show her taking a prominent role, but then Mac Cionnaith's fellow councillor who was given KPPS protection was also not prominent in meetings when he attended.

Phillips then said that Operation Fagotto, an operation run by RUC Special Branch that had been carried out in the vicinity of Rosemary Nelson's home on the weekend immediately before her murder on Monday, 15 March 1999, would be looked into. He said that, for Operation Fagotto to be of interest to the inquiry, there would have to be a link between police activity that weekend and the bomb being put on the underside of Rosemary Nelson's car. For this reason, the inquiry would have to decide if the bomb was attached before the weekend (Rosemary was on holiday and had taken the car with her) or on the eve of her murder, when her BMW was parked outside her house all night. There was also the question as to whether the heightened police activity had been a way of allowing the bomb to be planted or a hindrance to terrorists operating.

He concluded the day's hearing by saying that the main focus of the inquiry would be the night of Sunday, 14 March 1999, the eve of Rosemary's murder. Phillips said that four key areas needed examination: (i) the vehicle checkpoint on nearby Castor Bay Road; (ii) a man in a balaclava allegedly climbing into a police Land Rover; (iii) the movements of two helicopters; and (iv) other allegations of security force activity from witnesses recorded by the Pat Finucane Centre.

On Day 15 of the hearings, evidence was heard from a witness who worked part-time at Rosemary Nelson's legal practice doing the accounting. Nuala McCann spoke about one of Rosemary's most prominent clients, Colin Duffy. McCann said that, before Rosemary's murder, she had never felt at risk because of her boss's defending of Duffy, and that it was only after Rosemary's murder that the office had begun to receive death threats that she started to feel concerned. (Rosemary had only told one or two trusted members of staff about the death threats she had received prior to her murder, so to most of the office staff, the death threats that were received after her death were a new thing.) She told how Duffy was not treated any differently to any other client, although, as she sat at the back of the office, she could not say for sure how often Duffy came into the office.

Evidence about a controversial point then arose, regarding the lease of a house to Colin Duffy that Rosemary Nelson owned. McCann said that Rosemary had planned to buy houses for each of her three children as they grew older, and that there was nothing strange about the temporary lease of one of them to Duffy. Although the lease of the house was not a topic of conversation among office staff, she said that she believed that nobody thought the arrangement out of the ordinary. However, after Rosemary's murder, she began to hear rumours of an affair between Rosemary and Colin Duffy. This rumour would continue to come up in the hearings.

Moving on to Rosemary Nelson's representation of the GRRC, McCann stated that Rosemary had only represented them because she had gone to school with the GRRC leader, Breandan Mac Cionnaith. She said that the practice's work with the GRRC was seasonal and focused on the period before the annual controversial marches on 12 July, and the complaints that came because of them. Staying with the GRRC, McCann told how she had seen Rosemary on the morning after she had allegedly been assaulted by RUC officers on the Garvaghy Road, and that Rosemary had been shaken and had bruises on her left thigh, arm and shoulder. McCann said that she had advised Rosemary to take photographs of her bruising as evidence, but that her boss had not done so.

McCann said that it was after the alleged Garvaghy Road assault that Rosemary's relations with the RUC worsened, and, from then until Rosemary's murder, the number of complaints made against the RUC accelerated. McCann added that it was no secret generally that Rosemary was not liked by the RUC, and that her boss had felt uncomfortable whenever she had to go to the Lurgan RUC station. The witness then spoke about the only time that she saw a threatening letter (as detailed earlier in this book) – the 'republican bastard... RIP' letter. When she had asked Rosemary if she was frightened, Rosemary had been relaxed in her response, although McCann thought that this was a 'front', but that it might have been possible that Rosemary thought that she would never really be targeted because she was a woman with children. She continued by saying that she never felt that her boss was gravely under threat, as Rosemary only represented her clients professionally and did not sympathise with their political causes or actions. She explained this by referring to how 'open' Rosemary's home was, and that she or others could pop into Rosemary's house by the back door.

McCann then said that Rosemary had become more concerned for her own safety after GRRC leader Mac Cionnaith had obtained a security device to enable him to check if his car had been tampered with. She had suggested to Rosemary that she should get one as well, and Rosemary had tried to do so, but failed and her home and office remained as 'open' as before. McCann added that she thought that Rosemary would have taken the advice if the RUC had suggested security measures about her car, home and movements.

One specific incident was then related, when Rosemary's guard had been dropped, and she showed real fear. It was in 1999 when the GRRC was meeting with the Orange Order, and the Orange Order were unhappy about her attendance at the discussions. McCann said that her boss had said to her, 'They are going to do a Pat Finucane on me.'

McCann told the hearing that she had arranged the service on Rosemary's new silver BMW just ten days before her murder, the first time it had been serviced. The garage staff had concentrated on a problem with the car's alarm system, and McCann said that she had not known the garage staff before. When asked about her memories of the murder itself, McCann said that Rosemary had phoned her when she got back from her weekend in Donegal on the Sunday evening before her murder. She added that a car belonging to a friend of Rosemary's had been parked in her boss's driveway for the whole weekend. When Phillips asked McCann what she remembered had happened to Rosemary's handbag straight after her murder, McCann recounted that Rosemary's husband Paul had picked it up and given it to her to look after. She had given it to her husband, who then passed it on to Rosemary's sister Bernie.

The next witness called was Mary Loughran, Rosemary Nelson's receptionist since early 1998 (although she had joined the firm in January 1994), who had worked for Rosemary's practice until six months after her boss's murder. Loughran began by saying that, when she joined the practice, the workload had mainly been regarding matrimonial cases and conveyancing work rather than criminal cases. She also said that, because the offices on William Street, Lurgan, were at the Catholic end of town, the majority of the clients were Catholic, but that there were Protestant members of staff and that clients would be taken on regardless of persuasion.

Loughran said that the first high-profile client that she remembered was Colin Duffy, and that a lawyer–client relationship between Rosemary and Duffy was already established when she joined the firm in January 1994.

She told the hearing that many other lawyers would not have taken Duffy on as a client because of his Republican background, even then. After Duffy became a client, she said that anyone with a complaint against the authorities began to come to Rosemary's firm. She also said that, when Duffy's first case had finished and he was released from prison, he continued to come to the office at least twice a week, without an appointment, and that Duffy would be given priority to see Rosemary. Loughran said that this had caused problems for her, as the waiting room was always very busy, and some were forced to wait standing.

Loughran said that the death threats to Rosemary had increased in 1997 as the GRRC workload increased with the growing marching disputes. She agreed with Phillips when he suggested that from about this time Rosemary's firm began to be seen as a Republican practice and Rosemary as a Republican lawyer. She added that, as the complaints came flooding in, members of the GRRC tended to take advantage of Rosemary's enthusiasm to help, and called on her at any time of the day or night. Loughran then spoke about two threatening phone calls to the office, which were detailed earlier in this book, but that Rosemary generally remained calm.

However, she then spoke about an incident that happened in October or November 1997. A bomb scare had meant that the whole of William Street where Rosemary's offices were based was evacuated, apart from Rosemary's firm, until one of their clients alerted them and they left the building. When Rosemary had asked RUC officers why her offices had not been warned of the danger, they apparently shrugged.

The final witness called that day was Emmet Sheridan, whose wife Annette worked for Rosemary's firm, and they both mixed with Rosemary and her family socially, too. Sheridan told the hearing that Rosemary represented clients from both sides of the community, and even handled divorces for policemen. He said that his wife would do small jobs for Rosemary, but that she had refused to measure the feet of someone accused of a terrorist offence as she had not wanted to give evidence in a potential terrorist case. However, Rosemary had persuaded her to do so, with the witness helping his wife. When asked if his wife had contributed money to Colin Duffy's bail, Emmet Sheridan said that he did not know of any request to do so, and that he would not have been happy if his wife had got involved in the matter.

Sheridan said that he had talked to Rosemary about her relationship with the RUC at Christmas 1997 at a bar during a firm social gathering. He said that Rosemary had said, 'Have you no television, Emmet? They're going to get me,' and that she had also told him that Sir Ronnie Flanagan hated her. This was the first time that Rosemary had spoken to him of her fears openly. On the same occasion, when Rosemary was asked who she could ask for help, she had said, 'Well, there isn't anybody.' When prompted, Sheridan said that having an RUC officer acting as security at her home was not possible after the alleged assault by the RUC on the Garvaghy Road, when Sheridan said that Rosemary had been pushed to the ground. Sheridan concluded by saying that Rosemary would almost always keep her worries to herself, but that his wife had noticed that the stress had caused Rosemary to lose weight, and that it had a negative impact on her family and social life.

Day 20 of the RNI hearings saw Colin Wells, a British diplomat, give evidence. He focused on the report into alleged intimidation of Northern Ireland lawyers compiled by the UN Special Rapporteur Param Cumaraswamy. He spoke about Cumaraswamy's remit and conduct of the investigation and said that he was a good Special Rapporteur. He explained that he had received a phone call from the NIO, who were relaying the concerns of Sir Ronnie Flanagan's office regarding comments that Flanagan had allegedly made and were to go into the report. These were about the comments discussed earlier about some Northern Ireland lawyers having sympathies for or even working for paramilitary groups. The Chief Constable's office wanted the report amended and the comments removed, as the Chief Constable denied making the comment in which some lawyers were named and said that its inclusion could potentially put the lives of the lawyers in danger. As we know, Cumaraswamy and his assistant were sure that the comments had been made but, in the end, the Special Rapporteur's office agreed to remove them to show goodwill.

Next to give evidence was Rosemary's youngest brother, Eunan Magee (13 years her junior). Magee explained that Rosemary had been the fourth of seven children in a working-class family, and that their father had worked in a factory while their mother was a housewife who looked after the children. They had been brought up strongly Catholic, he said. He added that he and Rosemary mutually knew each other's friends as they were a close family, and that he was very grateful to his sister, as she had lent him her car when he was young and helped him out financially. He went on to talk about the birthmark that Rosemary had been born with on her face, her numerous skin-grafting operations and the resulting paralysis on one side of her face. He strongly refuted the allegation that Rosemary had been a bomber and that her disfigurement was a result of an explosion she was caught in.

Eunan Magee said that he did not have so much contact with his sister after he moved away from Lurgan in 1995. He said that it was the Colin Duffy case that first made his sister more high profile, that he had sometimes seen her on television regarding Duffy, and also that Duffy had asked for her representation because she was talented and approachable. But he added that Rosemary also had Unionist clients, and that his sister had been full of horror when the prominent Loyalist and LVF paramilitary leader Billy Wright was murdered in prison in December 1997.

Magee then spoke of Rosemary's professional reputation in Lurgan, and that she was well thought of due to the high quality of her work and the dedicated way that she represented her clients. He added that she did favours for her clients free and that she would be approached for advice when out socially. He gave an example of her generosity as when she had given a local man with an alcohol problem money for a taxi to Portadown. However, he said that people who were not from Lurgan might only have known Rosemary for her high-profile cases and their coverage in the media.

He also explained how he became concerned with his

sister's involvement in the controversial Garvaghy Road disputes and that, in summer 1997, their sister Bernie was so concerned that she had called Rosemary asking her to come home from the Garvaghy Road. But Rosemary had refused.

He said that his sister was politically engaged, but that she had taken on representing the GRRC because she thought that their civil rights were being abused. She was also an enthusiastic supporter of the Good Friday Agreement, and that politically she did what she thought was right, even voting for a Unionist politician once because she agreed with what he stood for. Her brother added that he would have been 'flabbergasted' if Rosemary had been connected in any way with paramilitary violence.

Regarding the threats to his sister, Magee stated that she thought she could protect herself by speaking of the threats publicly, but that she would have taken RUC security advice if it were from a high level. He expanded on this by saying that Rosemary's relations with the RUC had not always been negative. At one stage in the early 1990s, he had been worried that she was too friendly with a police officer who came from a different community but, by the middle 1990s, she was marked out as a Republican. He added that, in the late 1990s, he had been in a Belfast bar talking to a stranger who spoke Gaelic, and who had told him that Colin Duffy had been 'stood down', meaning that Duffy had been in a paramilitary group but had been taken out of service. Rosemary Nelson was still representing Duffy at this time.

He added that, by the late 1990s, Rosemary 'began to realise that she was fighting a lonely battle representing certain people', and that his family knew that these clients were seriously emotionally draining for his sister, as she would always give everything she had and also be friends to them. He said that his instinct told him that, in the last months of her life, Rosemary was trying to rebalance her life, to give more time to her husband and three children. He added that she was 'living on her nerves' and nicotine and caffeine.

Magee was direct in saying that Rosemary had turned into 'a hate figure' for some people because of her representation of convicted terrorists. Some people on the Loyalist side identified her with the causes of her clients, and not just as their lawyer, and this put her at risk. He added that his sister would have seen herself as a Nationalist interested in Irish culture, and that her Unionist clients accepted that without thinking.

Talking about the weekend before his sister's murder, he said that he had been at home while Rosemary had gone to her mobile home in Bundoran, Donegal. On the Sunday, he had driven past his sister's home at about 6.00pm and looked to see if she was home, but she was not. He added that he had not noticed any unusual security activity in the area that day as many others had.

He then spoke about the murder investigation, led by Colin Port, saying that Port had opened up a communication channel with Rosemary's family (parents, brothers and sisters) as they had not received as much information as Rosemary's widower Paul. Eunan Magee said that he thought that the identity of Rosemary's killers was probably already known by the RUC before Colin Port came to Northern Ireland from Norfolk. He believed this because the LVF was so very heavily infiltrated by the security services, but that this was his view and could not be substantiated.

Magee ended his evidence that day by saying that his family was Nationalist, but had no political agenda, and that they just wanted to discover the circumstances that had allowed Rosemary's murder to happen. He added that his family had been positive about the murder investigation, aiding Colin Port to approach witnesses, and that they had no interest in a negative outcome so they 'could bash the system'. He then said that all his family wished to know from the inquiry was 'who the perpetrators were, if there was inaction, what inaction there was and who is going to be accountable as a result'.

On Day 23 of the hearings, Patrick Vernon, a solicitor at Rosemary Nelson's practice (there were only two solicitors in the 1990s – Vernon and Nelson), gave his evidence. Speaking about the personal security of one of his clients, Vernon said that he had put in a request for his client to be dropped outside Lurgan RUC station when he was released, so that his family could pick him up. This request is put into perspective when we remember the murder of Sam Marshall upon leaving Lurgan RUC station in 1990, covered earlier in this book. The client had been held at Castlereagh holding centre, and Vernon said that such requests were made by either himself or Rosemary Nelson.

The inquiry then heard that Rosemary had visited both Lurgan RUC station and Castlereagh holding centre often in February 1998, but that this was not surprising as she and Patrick Vernon were the only staff authorised to do so as solicitors. Vernon told the hearing that Rosemary would try to avoid attending police stations and holding centres (for reasons we heard earlier), but that, if he was tied up, she would go.

Vernon then spoke about threatening calls to the legal practice. He mentioned the first call which he received, already covered by an earlier witness, when the caller, who had a thick Mid-Ulster accent, had said that the LVF would be present at a march in Portadown – one which Rosemary would attend, too. Vernon had told Rosemary about this call as he believed it to be serious, but she had laughed it off, even joking that she sometimes forgot to lock the back door of her house. Like an earlier witness and member of staff at Nelson's practice, Vernon had advised Rosemary to vary her routine, but she continued to park her car in the same space outside the office every day. Vernon had also received menacing calls after Rosemary's murder, the gist of which was usually the caller 'gloating' that Rosemary would never walk down the Garvaghy Road again. Vernon said that he always hung up when he realised what the nature of these calls was.

Vernon also said that an incident around Christmas 1998 had worried Rosemary more than the letter threats she had received. Detailed earlier in this book, this was when a car with four people inside had pulled up beside Rosemary in William Street car park and all stared at her in a sinister and threatening way which continued as the car slowly pulled away. Vernon also spoke about other threatening notes that Rosemary had received, many badly spelled, and that Rosemary had joked that she could not be scared of somebody who could not spell correctly. Vernon said that, in his opinion, Rosemary thought that such messages were only intended to frighten her, and not threats which would be carried out. On whether Rosemary had ever made concerted efforts to get security protection for herself, Vernon said that it was her staff who made efforts and suggestions in that direction, and not Rosemary herself.

When questioned about alleged RUC intimidation of his clients, Vernon said that such tactics would never have made his clients make false admissions, and that clients being investigated for alleged terrorist offences would mostly utilise their right to remain silent. Regarding whether Rosemary had a deep hatred of the RUC, Vernon said that he thought not, but that she had lost her respect for the police force because of the experiences of her clients and herself. Finally, Vernon said that he did not think that Rosemary filed the threats she received, but that she had normally thrown them away.

The next witness was Sir Louis Blom-Cooper, the first Independent Commissioner for Holding Centres, appointed in 1992, and who stayed in the post until April 1999, a month after Rosemary Nelson's murder. Blom-Cooper said that his remit was 'to provide further assurance to the Secretary of State that persons detained in the holding centres were fairly treated and that both statutory and administrative safeguards were being properly applied'. He added that he was not a Complaints Officer himself and that these had to be passed on to the RUC for investigation. He said that, in his opinion, there were no complaints of ill treatment of a detainee after he was appointed as the Independent Commissioner.

Blom-Cooper said that he had had 'minimal contact' with solicitors in his role, but that there had been unfounded rumours going around that solicitors who attended and worked in the holding centres were passing information to paramilitaries. He said that one law firm, Madden & Finucane (co-founded by Pat Finucane, who was murdered almost three years before Blom-Cooper took up his post), was under particular suspicion from the police because of its clients and the work it did. Blom-Cooper said that he had suggested a new proposal of having a duty solicitor at each holding centre to stop these rumours and suspicions, but that it had been vetoed by the Law Society as it would stop other lawyers (picked by clients) from getting work. He added that the RUC was usually receptive to his suggestions.

However, he said that the conditions at Castlereagh holding centre were terrible; the tiny size of the cells, the overall atmosphere and there being no exercise yard made it very oppressive for those held there. He also said that the 1994 ceasefires in Northern Ireland had resulted in a reduction of holding-centre use and also of suspicions of solicitors involved with paramilitaries. To illustrate the religious segregation in Northern Ireland, he remembered that a police officer had once asked him if he was a Jewish Protestant or a Jewish Catholic.

Speaking about Rosemary Nelson, Blom-Cooper said that in his opinion the way in which she operated was not wise, as she was usually alone dealing with controversial legal issues. He added that he had become increasingly aware of RUC hostility towards Rosemary, and that the fact that she was a woman and a single practitioner at the holding centres might have been one of the reasons for this. Recalling that he had received a letter stating that Rosemary had been receiving death threats, he said that he had passed this on to the Attorney General, as dealing with it was outside his remit. He went on to say that his working relationship with the RUC Chief Constable was 'excellent'. However, Sir Ronnie Flanagan was disapproving of the use of audio and video recording of the interrogations of detainees or the RUC being researched by him or academics, as this could hinder the questioning of suspects.

On Day 30, 5 June 2008, the UN Special Rapporteur Param Cumaraswamy was heard. He said how he had met between 20 and 30 Northern Ireland lawyers, all of whom had claimed that they had suffered intimidation and harassment, usually through their clients, the gist of which being that their lawyers would get into 'further trouble'. Cumaraswamy noted that there was a systematic manner to the threats, but that Rosemary Nelson was the only lawyer who had received 'direct threats' at the time he was compiling his report for the UN. He added that these lawyers did not usually make their complaints through the normal system – through the RUC and the Law Society – as they had little confidence in the systems in place, and that complaints were normally made to NGOs (Amnesty International is an example). However, there had been complaints made about alleged harassment and intimidation of Rosemary Nelson through the system, though no action was taken on these.

Cumaraswamy told the hearing that, at a meeting with the RUC Chief Constable Sir Ronnie Flanagan, he had spoken about his concern regarding harassment and intimidation, and that Flanagan had denied the allegations completely. The UN Special Rapporteur then said that Flanagan had told him that the main desire of paramilitaries was to ensure that detainees remained silent, and that lawyers were involved in ensuring that occurred. Flanagan had added that, in his view, the solicitors concerned 'could' be working for paramilitary groups, thereby identifying the solicitors with the causes of their clients. Cumaraswamy then referred to a broadcaster, John Ware, who had made notes of an interview with Flanagan in preparation for a *Panorama* programme, and that Ware's notes reinforced what Flanagan had allegedly told Cumaraswamy. The witness said that Flanagan was of the opinion that there was a political agenda to paint the RUC as part of the Unionist tradition and that these allegations of RUC harassment and intimidation were part of that agenda. Cumaraswamy then said that the 'corruption' of solicitors was often referenced in his meeting with Flanagan, and that it was suggested that the Independent Commissioner for Holding Centres, Sir Louis Blom-Cooper, agreed with this view. We have already heard, though, that Blom-Cooper himself had said that there was no substantiation for these claims.

Cumaraswamy then detailed his only meeting with Rosemary Nelson on his Northern Ireland visit – no one else was present – when she had outlined the kind of alleged threats made against her and the alleged harassment and intimidation of other defence lawyers. Cumaraswamy said that he thought that Rosemary Nelson's case was more serious than those of other lawyers and that, in his opinion, she was targeted to stop her acting for her clients. Speaking about his second meeting with Rosemary in Washington, DC on 29 September 1998 at the Congressional Subcommittee meeting, the UN Special Rapporteur said that he spoke to Rosemary as part of a discussion panel, and that he got the impression that the alleged threats against her were continuing. He said that that was the last contact he had with her, as she was murdered less than six months later. He had issued a press release the day after her murder demanding an independent and impartial inquiry.

As we saw earlier in this book, a British Government Minister had made allegations that solicitors in Northern Ireland were working for or sympathising with paramilitary groups less than a month before the defence lawyer Pat Finucane was murdered. The RUC Chief Constable denied that he had repeated such allegations to Cumaraswamy, and Flanagan was concerned that, if the reports were included in Cumaraswamy's report, Rosemary's life could be in danger. As we also know, the names of these solicitors were removed from the report for this reason, after requests made by the British High Commission in Kuala Lumpur (where Cumaraswamy was based) and by Sir Ronnie Flanagan himself.

The next witness called to the hearing was Cumaraswamy's UN assistant Alan Parra, who said that their short visit to Northern Ireland had not been long enough to find the true answers to questions of harassment and intimidation of defence lawyers. He also said that some of the officials they met on the trip were not well briefed, particularly RUC Chief Constable Sir Ronnie Flanagan and the Independent Commissioner for Holding Centres, Sir Louis Blom-Cooper.

Parra spoke about the three solicitors outlined in the report, who included Rosemary Nelson. He went on to talk about the call he had received from Sir Ronnie

Flanagan himself asking for the reference to the solicitors to be removed, and that he denied making the comments about solicitors being involved with paramilitaries. Parra said that he had asked Flanagan what protection had been given to Rosemary Nelson by the RUC, and Flanagan had replied that Rosemary had been offered protection but declined to take it (although we know that Rosemary thought that the RUC was the source of most threats to her).

After outlining a second, much shorter call he had received from Flanagan on the issue, Parra told the hearing that Rosemary Nelson had been informed about the inclusion of her name in the UN report. However, she had wanted her name to remain in it, as she felt that it would give her some protection. Another of the three lawyers shared this view. But, as we know, the names and reference were cut from the report in the end.

On 16 June 2008, a witness was questioned by the Counsel to the Inquiry, Mr Savill, about a statement he had given to the inquiry on 2 April that year. His name was Gary Martin Marshall, and he had been arrested and held by the RUC on 21 February 1997 about a murder. Savill told the hearing that Rosemary Nelson had been Marshall's lawyer and that Marshall had repeatedly refused to sign RUC custody records and other documents as he did not trust the RUC. Marshall had made contact with Rosemary around ten times before the 21 February 1997 arrest, regarding 'civil and criminal matters'. After that arrest, Marshall was held at the Castlereagh holding centre, and was released six days later on 27 February 1997. Marshall informed the inquiry that he could not remember much of the interviews conducted by the RUC during his detention (it was over 11 years earlier). However, he did remember that his lawyer Rosemary Nelson had been threatened through him and that nasty remarks about her facial paralysis had been made, although he could not remember exactly what was said.

Marshall told the inquiry that, on the Monday after his arrest, Rosemary had visited him in his cell. At this stage, he did not report any complaints, with Rosemary just drafting Marshall's statement as to his alibi at the time of the murder, which she took down by hand. After Rosemary had left, RUC officers told him that his detention was going to be extended, as they had received an order to do so. Two days later, Marshall received two visits in his cell – one from Rosemary at lunchtime and the other in the evening from a solicitor at her practice, Patrick Vernon. By this time, the RUC had issued Marshall with a written caution. At this time, Marshall complained that the RUC officers were writing down questions, but not asking him them.

Inquiry Counsel Savill then referred to a 26 February 1998 statement made by a Castlereagh RUC sergeant, stating that the officer had asked the witness (Marshall) if he wanted to make a written statement about the allegations being made against him about the murder. According to the sergeant's statement, Marshall declined, but had then given a verbal statement saying that detectives had said that Rosemary Nelson was giving him the wrong advice. When questioned about this by Savill, Marshall told the hearing that he could not remember the visit to his cell by the sergeant, or the comments made by the detectives saying that Rosemary was giving him the wrong advice.

Savill then went into details about the statement made by Marshall a few days after his release on 27 February 1997. Marshall told the hearing that this statement could be relied on. It largely referred to comments allegedly made to Marshall during his detention by RUC officers, which were mentioned earlier in this book. Savill read out parts of the statement to the hearing. Referring to 27 February 1997, the day of his release, Marshall had stated that RUC detectives had said 'that the IRA had given her [Rosemary Nelson] the statement which I had given them. They said the IRA were pulling her strings. They also said there was a new law passed in 1989 which meant they could do away with solicitors who concocted stories.'

Continuing to read from Marshall's statement, Savill said, '"There was then another interview after lunchtime. It was the same two detectives, and the tall one said to me that he heard I had been making complaints. He said that this has been going on for 30 years and it was not going to change now. He said to tell 'half-face' that. They said I made the statement and Rosemary got the witnesses and told them what to say."'

Later, Savill made reference to the 'Statement of Gary Marshall', given to the CAJ's then legal officer Paul Mageean in Rosemary Nelson's offices on 5 March 1998. Savill pointed out that the main complaint made by Marshall in the statement was the length of his time in detention. Savill said that it was curious that this should be the main complaint as there had allegedly been so many nasty remarks made about Marshall himself and his lawyer Rosemary Nelson. Marshall replied that, as he had already reported those remarks to Rosemary, he had expected her to take that matter further anyway, and that his duty was only to report them to her. He also added that he had not wanted any further involvement with the RUC.

Savill rounded off the day's hearing by referring to a statement that Marshall made to the Pat Finucane Centre on 24 March 1999, nine days after Rosemary Nelson's murder. Savill pointed out that the witness had signed this statement, while the one given to Paul Mageean just over a year before was not signed. Marshall could not give any reason why this was so, but said that the earlier statement given to Paul Mageean closer to the events was more reliable. Marshall added that derogatory remarks about Rosemary Nelson were also made on other occasions he was arrested. Sir Nicholas Burden, an Inquiry Panel Member, then asked Marshall why he thought these alleged threats were made to Rosemary Nelson and himself, and Marshall replied that they were personal attacks, in his opinion.

On 24 June 2008, Day 40, Rory Phillips QC, Leading Counsel for the Inquiry, began to outline Part 2 of the 'Bundle' material. The focus for this part of the inquiry was: (i) at what level Rosemary Nelson was of interest to the intelligence agencies and why; (ii) how this intelligence was dispersed among agencies and how much for each of them; (iii) how this intelligence affected the perception of Rosemary in the security forces and other agencies; (iv) the amount of intelligence about her that was known outside of the intelligence agencies and State departments and if this affected her safety; and (v) if there was any intelligence regarding threats to Rosemary that could lead to who was responsible for her murder.

Phillips added that the matter of the influence of

intelligence gathered on Rosemary Nelson also had to be considered in the context of her murder and the murder investigation, and the effect it had on the attitudes of the RUC and Special Branch. Had it led to 'something less than full co-operation' with the murder investigation? Had there been information held back from the murder investigation team as it was thought exposure of it could put sources of intelligence at risk? He said that the three main contributors of the intelligence material on Rosemary Nelson in Part 2 of the inquiry were the PSNI – which also incorporated the material given by its predecessor, the RUC – the Security Service and the Army. Phillips said that he would look at how the Rosemary Nelson intelligence came to the interest of the intelligence agencies and he would also refer to the intelligence given to the inquiry on the three principal Loyalist paramilitaries operating when Rosemary was murdered in March 1999.

Phillips then detailed the structure of law enforcement and counter-terrorism up to and at the time of Rosemary Nelson's murder, and at the time that the inquiry was gathering intelligence on her from the agencies as evidence. He pointed out that, after 1976, RUC Special Branch had been in control of intelligence and counter-terrorism operations in Northern Ireland, but that, from October 2007 (at the time the RNI was gathering evidence), the responsibility had been passed to the Security Service. As detailed earlier, the role of MI5 in the inquiry and its overall responsibility for intelligence about Rosemary Nelson had greatly concerned her family and many prominent people, as some felt that key intelligence could be suppressed for security reasons.

Phillips then went into the structure of the RUC, saying that it had been organised along military lines, to a larger extent than the majority of other police forces. The Chief Constable at the time of Rosemary's murder, Sir Ronnie Flanagan, was, of course, the head of the hierarchy and, just under him, the Assistant Chief Constable was the head of Special Branch, known as the HSB. He added that, in the late 1990s, Special Branch comprised of 850 officers, around 10 per cent of the whole RUC. Special Branch had had a complex structure with many subsections and had been described in a report as 'a force within a force'. Specifically, section E9 was in charge of operations, including surveillance, especially on Republicans.

Phillips then referred to a surveillance operation carried out on the Mid-Ulster LVF (then led by Mark Fulton) which started in April 1998, and was run by Special Branch and the Army. The details of the operation, called Operation Shubr, had been retrieved from the PSNI's database. An intelligence report on the operation stated that 'Mid-Ulster LVF have some form of terrorist activity planned for the near future'. Operation Shubr would carry on until August 2000, but intelligence reports from April–October 1998 (a year to six months before Rosemary Nelson's murder) showed that Mark Fulton and his LVF activities in Portadown were the chief target of the surveillance. It transpired that Operation Shubr was in action on some dates in March 1999, but was not active on the weekend immediately before Rosemary's murder on Monday, 15 March. Phillips said that, as the LVF were suspected of committing Rosemary's murder, and that key members of the group had been the targets of the surveillance operation, this posed questions.

As the hearings heard at the beginning, Operation Fagotto was also being run by RUC Special Branch. This was the cause of much of the security activity around Rosemary Nelson's home on the weekend and especially the evening before her murder, which Rosemary herself had even commented on in a telephone call that evening. Phillips said that intelligence showed that this was a long-term operation, and not just active that weekend, and that the surveillance target was an individual suspected of being involved significantly in Provisional IRA activity in the south of Ireland. Phillips next said that the inquiry also had to ask about how often the RUC Chief Constable was briefed about operations such as Shubr and Fagotto, and who briefed him. Phillips said that the inquiry had been given little evidence as to these issues.

The next agency considered was the Army. Phillips said that the British Army had first been sent to Northern Ireland when the Troubles began in 1969 (to help the RUC), and that they had remained operational there until July 2007, almost four decades later. He said that in the late 1990s there were around 9,000 soldiers in Northern Ireland, in addition to the 4,500 troops of the RIR. Phillips said that at this time the Army identified its role as supporting the RUC, and this included everyday tasks, such as checkpoints, patrols and public order back-up, but also more focused support, such as bomb disposal and the use of army helicopters. He added that the Army also had an intelligence role, and this was the reason for many of the witness statements in relation to the extraordinary amount of security force activity close to Rosemary's Lurgan home on the weekend before her murder.

Phillips referred to a document regarding military deployments in the period 1–14 March 1999. This was Operation Improvise, which had been active 43 times in the first half of 1999, including on the weekend immediately before Rosemary's murder. The hearing then heard that one of the key questions was how intelligence on Rosemary Nelson had been shared between the Army (the MoD) and the RUC.

Attention was then turned to the role of the Security Services in Rosemary Nelson's case. Phillips said that the paramount role of the Security Services in Northern Ireland was to assess and distribute all intelligence gathered from operations. This Assessment Group provided assessment and strategic intelligence reports to the British Government, known as Northern Ireland Intelligence Reports (NIIRs). Operationally, the Security Services ran sources and agents in Northern Ireland, and some officers gave support to the RUC in the areas of eavesdropping and bugging surveillance operations. Apparently, the Security Service had told the inquiry that the RUC chose the targets for eavesdropping, and that it supplied technical and logistical support in the installing and maintenance of devices.

Regarding Rosemary Nelson, Phillips returned to a key point that he had mentioned at the very beginning of the hearings in his opening address, the subject of there being no paper file on Rosemary Nelson submitted by the PSNI as evidence to the inquiry. Indeed, the PSNI had told the inquiry that it had not held (or the RUC had not held) a paper file on Rosemary Nelson before her murder.

Phillips stated that there were a number of early intelligence reports on Rosemary Nelson, gathered by RUC Special Branch. In December 1994, for example, Rosemary was reported as creating a false alibi for Colin Duffy, suspected of being a member of the Provisional IRA, who was then in custody on remand for the murder of part-time UDR soldier John Lyness. And, in April 1996, there were three reports on Rosemary, one of which reported that she was using her position as a lawyer to collect information for the Provisional IRA in Lurgan, including the personal details of RUC officers whom she met. Another stated that 'Nelson is known to represent a number of Republican activists in the Lurgan area' and that 'she would take a very keen interest with the Republican movement and especially Sinn Fein whom she legally represents'.

Phillips summarised by saying that it was certain that three types of intelligence had been collected about Rosemary Nelson since 1996. These were that she was alleged to have had an association with the Lurgan Provisional IRA (including with its suspected leader Colin Duffy), her association with the GRRC, and more personal intelligence about her political associations, friends and family. From this material, Phillips said that it could be suggested that, if this intelligence from 1994–96 was thought to be reliable by RUC Special Branch, then the idea that Rosemary was an active supporter of 'military or militant Republicanism' could already have been ingrained. Phillips said that this perception that she was active would have been fuelled by two factors: her helping Duffy get off and allegedly aiding the Lurgan Provisional IRA to target RUC officers. He added that the intelligence gathered in those reports must be read in a balanced way, especially bearing in mind the anti-RUC publicity created by Rosemary's successful representation of Duffy in his appeal against conviction for the murder of John Lyness.

Staying with Rosemary's client Colin Duffy, Phillips then focused on Duffy's arrest on 23 June 1997 on suspicion of the murder of two Lurgan RUC officers. Within weeks, RUC Special Branch started intelligence reporting on Rosemary Nelson's part in the legal case, and this would continue for the whole of 1998. Reading from these reports, Phillips said that Rosemary was reported as continuing her support for Provisional IRA members. He added that it was not known just how widely this intelligence was passed outside Special Branch, and if it might have affected her safety. Phillips continued that a number of reports from November 1997 focused on Rosemary's role in gaining publicity for the alleged harassment of Colin Duffy by the RUC. One report quoted said, 'It is believed that Rosemary Nelson is making plans for Colin Duffy to take part in a Channel 4 documentary which will investigate police harassment of Republicans in the Lurgan area.' There was also a reference to 'a propaganda war' against the security forces in relation to the alleged harassment of Duffy.

Phillips said that all of these incidents got considerable political and media attention, which were now a subject of discussion in the top levels of the NIO and the RUC (including the Chief Constable). In addition, the Director of BIRW, Jane Winter, was also getting involved in matters involving Rosemary Nelson, as was Mo Mowlam and the DPP.

The next item on the agenda was the intelligence relating to the alleged personal relationship between Rosemary Nelson and Colin Duffy. This was reported as having started in late 1997, and a February 1998 report stated that they were still having a 'close, intimate relationship', seeing each other almost daily. This intelligence reporting continued to October 1998 (five months before Rosemary's murder) and was a basis for an application for the subsequent Operation Indus. Intelligence reported that Duffy had been seen driving Rosemary's car on more than one occasion. Phillips said that, from this intelligence, Special Branch officers might have inferred that Rosemary and Duffy were engaged in a sexual relationship, but that it was not known who suspected this. He then made it clear that evidence heard at the inquiry about this sensitive allegation was only heard in relation to how this could have affected perceptions of Rosemary Nelson and if it affected her safety.

Phillips then looked at Operation Indus, which was a technical operation applied for by Lurgan RUC Special Branch (and also seen by the Security Service) in August 1998, the purpose of which was an attack on the house owned by Rosemary and leased to Colin Duffy. The application for Operation Indus followed the controversial events around Drumcree in the previous month. An intelligence report from this time stated that 'Nelson uses her legal training to assist PIRA in any way she can. It is clear that Nelson is a dedicated Republican.'

Following that, Phillips turned to the more personal intelligence that had been gathered about Rosemary Nelson. This included her relations with the family of the murdered Robert Hamill, her family and social life, professional, religious and political associations and her contacts with politicians and NGOs (for instance, British Human Rights Watch and Amnesty International). Phillips then put it to the inquiry: if there was such personal intelligence gathered, could it be assumed that there was a file on Rosemary Nelson at the time of her murder? He also asked if there had been any intelligence about threats to her or her murder that had not been disclosed to the inquiry, or if intelligence of this had been received, but not recorded by Special Branch, or even if it had been reported but later erased from databases.

And on this point, on 28 July 2008, the *Belfast Telegraph* claimed that a Loyalist called Trevor McKeown, serving life in Maghaberry Prison for the murder of 18-year-old Bernadette Martin, had alleged that RUC officers had asked him to shoot Rosemary Nelson dead less than two years before she was murdered. He said that, while he was being interrogated in July 1997 about Bernadette Martin's murder, RUC officers had taken him to where Rosemary usually parked her car and encouraged him to shoot her there. McKeown said, 'When I was arrested, a detective said to me, "You shouldn't have killed that 18-year-old, but Rosemary Nelson instead."'

Two English policemen had interviewed McKeown in prison about the allegations, which the RUC officers in question 'strenuously denied'. However, it was found that the same RUC officers had been involved in an internal RUC complaints investigation prompted by a complaint made by Rosemary Nelson herself years earlier. No evidence had been found to support the allegations, but McKeown was quoted as saying that he was prepared to give evidence at the RNI, but that he was worried about his safety if he did so.

In response to the allegations, Phillips said, 'Now, at present, it is not clear to what extent we will be able to explore this matter in the evidence... this was a matter again investigated by the murder investigation team; the allegations were denied and no charges were brought as a result. However, it was with these sorts of allegations in mind and as one of a series of measures designed to encourage witnesses to be open in their evidence to the inquiry and to ensure that the inquiry received the fullest disclosure and co-operation from those with material of relevance that the inquiry, during the course of 2005, sought from the then Attorney General, Lord Goldsmith, a limited evidential indertaking.' This 'undertaking' promised that anyone giving evidence could not be prosecuted on their own evidence in any other, later criminal case.

Day 46 of the hearings, heard on 8 September 2008, began with the witness David Nairn, who had worked in several sections of the RUC. He reached the rank of Chief Inspector in the Complaints and Discipline Department from September 1998 until 2001, when the RUC was disbanded and succeeded by the PSNI. Therefore, he was in charge of a key department at a key time in the Rosemary Nelson case. The operational aspects of the RUC Complaints Department were covered earlier, so this will not be repeated here.

Nairn was asked about three complaints made by Rosemary Nelson, and outlined how they were dealt with. He told the hearing that he stood by a statement he had made to the inquiry saying that there was generally co-operation from the Unionist side when dealing with complaints. However, by the middle of November 1998, he had decided that Rosemary Nelson was not co-operative, but that he had no personal view of her. He said that he had been frustrated at this, not being able to investigate the complaints completely, but that he had not been 'hugely irritated'. He added that correspondence Rosemary had sent to his department was a waste of time, as there would be no result due to her lack of co-operation. But he said that he had felt no animosity towards Rosemary, and that his view of her did not influence his work, in his opinion, and that he followed procedures and did everything he could to get her to give evidence.

Regarding the third complaint, received by letter on 23 October 1998, there was an internal RUC memo stating that the complaint could not be sorted out informally because of Rosemary's attitude to the security services, but Nairn said that he had never talked about her attitude with colleagues.

The next witness was Norman McKee, who had been a member of the RUC since May 1984, later working in the CID Department in Portadown for four years, and in 1997 he was the head of a mobile support unit (MSU), containing four sergeants and twenty officers, using Land Rovers. The role of the MSU was to calm public disorder. McKee said that his CID role involved very little contact with RUC Special Branch, and that, when he took charge of the MSU in July 1997, the Drumcree Conflict was in full swing. But he said that his only prior knowledge of the GRRC was from the media and common knowledge.

Regarding the murder of the two RUC officers in June 1997, McKee said that most of his colleagues thought that the local IRA had carried it out, but that he had held no personal view (these were the murders that Colin Duffy was pulled in for). However, he was aware that Duffy was the chief suspect, and that Rosemary Nelson represented him, as well as the fact that Rosemary and Duffy had an acquaintance, but that he did not know what kind of acquaintanceship.

The focus then moved on to RUC deployment in Drumcree on 6 July 1997, and McKee said that several hundred members of the security services had been drafted in. He said that, on that day, Rosemary Nelson had approached him at about 6.00am and had asked to speak to his superior officer. He said that Rosemary did not seem agitated or tense. Rosemary Nelson would later make a complaint about that day, saying that RUC officers had called her 'a Fenian bitch' and told her to 'fuck off', as well as spitting at her. McKee said that he saw none of these incidents and, as he had tried to find his superior officer, she had not mentioned that she wanted to file a complaint. He then described the riot gear used by the RUC that day, and he said that the balaclava reached the nose, and therefore it was not possible to spit with one on. McKee added that he had no further dealings with Rosemary Nelson personally.

On 16 September 2008, the RNI heard from Eamon Stack, who continued his evidence about Rosemary Nelson's work with the GRRC. He said that she worked for them on a *pro bono* basis. Then he spoke about an event on the Garvaghy Road on the night of 5 July 1997, the day before the incident that the witness Norman

McKee of the RUC had spoken of, in which Rosemary Nelson had alleged that RUC officers abused her. At the event the night before, Stack said that some teenagers were carrying out a sit-down, a kind of peaceful protest, and that there were around 150 people sitting down on the road.

He added that the protesters had co-operated with the police as they were taken off the road. However, Stack said that he had made a complaint because he alleged that an RUC officer had kicked a female protester in the thigh (he knew of other incidents, but this was the only one he had personally seen). He stated that the RUC officer had had no identification on his uniform, so the complaint could not be investigated, but he had made it to get his voice heard. Otherwise, he said, the GRRC had meetings with the RUC, and relations between them were professional but tense. Stack said that he could not remember seeing Rosemary Nelson there that night.

Stack then spoke about a 1997 telephone death threat received by Breandan Mac Cionnaith, the leader of the GRRC. He said that he had spoken to Mac Cionnaith about it and that, in his opinion, this threat had come from the LVF leader Billy Wright himself (who was murdered later that year). He said that he did not remember ever talking to Rosemary Nelson about her personal security. However, he added that everyone involved with the GRRC was potentially a target.

Next Alan Todd was heard. He was a member of the RUC from 1991, reaching the rank of Chief Superintendent. In 1997, he was a sergeant and working with the MSU. He said that his knowledge of Rosemary Nelson was very limited, but that he knew that she made police officers nervous as she was very focused. The attention then turned again to the night and early morning of 5–6 July 1997. Todd said that he had been hit by a brick on that night, but that he was not involved with removing protesters from the road. The hearing was shown the RUC helmet worn in 1997, and Todd said that officers would pull down the balaclava on it to speak to somebody, but that in 1997 there were no identity numbers on them.

Todd said that he saw Rosemary Nelson approaching that night with a group of Garvaghy Road residents whom she represented. He remembered that she was talking to RUC officers up and down the police cordon, and that she wanted to get through the cordon to speak to more of her clients. He said that she was a public figure and therefore had a special status. Todd said he had spoken to her, as he could see the situation was tense. Then he stated that Rosemary Nelson became angry and agitated when he told her she could not pass through the cordon, but that her clients were free to come and join her on that side if they wished. Todd added that no RUC officer present either physically or verbally abused her.

Todd told the hearing that he had encountered Rosemary once again in 1997 in Lurgan when his MSU was offering support to the local unit. In relation to the Nelson murder investigation, Todd admitted that he had been surprised about the RUC South Region's involvement in it as the majority of complaints filed by Rosemary were against South Region, but that he had full trust in the integrity of RUC officers.

The penultimate witness of the day was Susan McKay, a journalist on the *Sunday Tribune* (based in Dublin) from 1992 to 2004. She specialised in Northern Ireland politics and also wrote books on the subject. McKay said that she knew Rosemary professionally, but that they were friendly with each other. McKay said that Rosemary would supply her with useful background and context about opinions in the Nationalist community, and sometimes put her in contact with people.

McKay had reported on the 1997 Drumcree Conflict, and said that Rosemary had told her at the conflict in the early hours that she had been assaulted and that she was going to make a complaint to the RUC. However, McKay said that she had not seen the assault herself. McKay said that Rosemary had shown her arm to her, but that she had not seen any bruising. McKay stated that Rosemary's complaint was not taken seriously, and that the RUC was dismissive of Rosemary. She added that Rosemary was not confrontational, in her opinion. Regarding alleged death threats made to Rosemary, McKay said that Rosemary had not thought that the RUC was going to be helpful in investigating them, when they discussed the subject on the phone.

As a journalist, Susan McKay also had Loyalist contacts, and she said that some of them spoke violently about Rosemary Nelson, and that some Loyalist paramilitaries would make remarks like 'she will be killed'. But, naturally, as a journalist, she refused to name them. McKay added that some Loyalists hated Rosemary as she was very effective in her legal activities with the GRRC and was, in some ways, winning the legal war.

McKay also said that she knew that some RUC officers had had friendly relations with Loyalist paramilitary members and that, inside the Orange

Order, the general view was that the police were on their side. However, McKay said that she had no information that suggested the RUC facilitated Rosemary Nelson's murder, but that in her view the RUC treated Rosemary with a lack of respect.

Regarding the Red Hand Defenders, who had claimed responsibility for Rosemary Nelson's murder, McKay said that they were not an entity or group at all, but a name used as a front for claiming violent acts. In her view, the Red Hand Defenders were associated with the Orange Order, the UDA and the LVF.

The final witness of the day was Andrew Cully, a member of the RUC from 1976 until 2004. He became Deputy Subdivisional Commander in Portadown in 1995, and then moved to the RUC Complaints Department in February 1998. He said that he worked in Complaints for ten months and, during that time, dealt with around 100 complaints, and that 70–80 of them related to alleged assault during arrest. He told the hearing that he could not say if complaints were sometimes made to use up the time and resources of the RUC from criminal investigations, but he did say that one law firm (unnamed) did register complaints and then say that they did not want to proceed. He added that this made it possible to infer that such complainants did not have trust in the complaints procedure and had an anti-RUC agenda.

Day 60 of the hearings sat on 7 October 2008 and Simon Rogers of the NIO Police Division gave evidence about the August 1998 threat assessment carried out on Rosemary Nelson, seven months before her murder. Rogers was asked questions about correspondence of 6

August and a reply on 3 September 1998. An allegation had been made that Rosemary was a former bomber (an allegation we have heard before in relation to her partial facial paralysis). The reply did not address this allegation or the issue of her personal security, particularly in relation to the KPPS. Rogers said that the reply gave reassurance that the RUC knew of no specific threat to Rosemary Nelson and that this needed no further clarification. Then his reply to Paul Mageean of the CAJ was given to Rogers to remind himself of the contents. This letter was sent three weeks after the previous letter he had sent, and Rogers said that he had not acted urgently as no threat was thought to exist. Rogers also told the hearing that he had not informed Rosemary Nelson about the police threat assessment, but then she had also not contacted him.

Rogers said that Mo Mowlam had contacted him after Rosemary Nelson's murder requesting him to look into what was being done to make sure that the RUC knew how crucial the murder investigation would be. She said that it would have to be an extraordinary investigation, as an ordinary one would not have the required impartiality. Rogers said that Mo Mowlam remained interested in the progress of the murder investigation and that, in his view, the investigation had good communication channels. Rogers concluded his evidence by saying that he considered that the threats against Rosemary Nelson had been dealt with satisfactorily, and that there was no prejudice shown by the RUC in dealing with alleged threats.

The next witness was Christine Collins, Head of the NIO Police Division until September 1998. She had reported directly to the Senior Director, and was effectively the boss of the previous witness, Simon Rogers. The KPSS (part of the Police Division) reported directly to her. She said that political tensions in Northern Ireland had been high between 1995 and 1998, and that these tensions had remained after the Good Friday Agreement. Collins said that, during the Troubles, anyone who worked in the 'security sector' could be a target, but, after Pat Finucane's murder in 1989, many had wondered if this should have also been extended to defence lawyers. However, she said that Rosemary Nelson was the only other defence lawyer who had been killed or indeed attacked. She added that the word 'abrasive' would best describe the relations between the RUC and defence lawyers, but that she personally condemned any police officer for allegedly verbally abusing a lawyer through their client or allegedly threatening a lawyer through their client.

Collins stated that, as a rule, Security Branch did risk assessments and Special Branch did threat assessments (the PSNI being divided into the Security Branch and Special Branch). Collins was shown a May 1997 letter outlining advice to be passed to the British Ambassador to the United States regarding the escalation of the threats made to Rosemary Nelson and her corresponding mounting fears. The witness told the hearing that the volume of paperwork relating to Rosemary Nelson started to grow from the spring of 1997, and at this time a file on her 'would have been' opened. Collins added that this case was a unique one as she had never been involved in a case concerning threats to a defence lawyer before.

The contents of that letter and one from a Mr Lynch of

the Lawyers Alliance received on 13 March 1997 were spoken about at a meeting with the Deputy Under-Secretary. The issues discussed were: (i) the death threats – these were passed to the RUC; (ii) the problem of the complaints about security force interrogations; (iii) the KPPS angle and the protection of Rosemary Nelson; and (iv) the political factors and if the RUC should investigate its own officers – this was important as any outside officer drafted in would have to be sworn in as an RUC member as a matter of procedure.

A letter of 6 June 1997 referred to the fact that Rosemary Nelson had refused to be interviewed by the RUC regarding the threats and security. Rosemary had been given advice to make contact with her local Lurgan investigating officer (but it should be remembered here that Rosemary was very wary of contact with the RUC because of the alleged threats she claimed RUC officers had made against her). Collins said that she was certain that there was no specific threat against Rosemary at that time, as otherwise a special procedure would have been used. She added that the correspondence had come from third parties and, as Rosemary would not be interviewed, it could not be ascertained if she actually was in fear of her life. The witness did admit that the correspondence did not answer a fundamental question: if the RUC had contacted Rosemary about her personal security or not. Collins stated that the implication was that the RUC had not contacted her, as Rosemary had not come forward herself and there was no evidence of a specific threat against her.

After speaking about the complaints coming out of the arrest of Colin Duffy in the summer of 1997, Collins was asked to focus on the correspondence of NGOs, particularly that from BIRW and the CAJ. Collins said that each complaint was dealt with seriously and thoroughly. But she did say that, after a meeting with the Lawyers Alliance in February 2008, she had recognised the high level of emotion about the Rosemary Nelson complaints. She added that, in her view, the RUC should have been vigilant about Rosemary as she was by now a high-profile public figure. She also said that the real reason why the complaints were being received from NGOs and not the normal channels was that Rosemary thought the system corrupt, that she really did have fears, but that there was no real danger to her from the RUC in reality.

On Day 78, 24 November 2008, the hearing heard from David Watkins, a civil servant and Director of Policing and Security (1998–2004). Watkins said that he had dealt with strategic intelligence that was not personalised, with no names included. However, he said that he was aware of the allegations made that the RUC had threatened Rosemary Nelson through her clients and that he thought he remembered her name coming up in a Security Policy meeting focused on the Drumcree Conflict, before her murder. He said that he had also known of the allegations made against Rosemary Nelson, but that he had never found any evidence to substantiate them. He had never asked for further information on Rosemary Nelson as he had had no reason to, he said.

While being questioned, Watkins remembered that some RUC officers held 'a pretty dim view' of Rosemary which he had gleaned from his talks with them over Drumcree, and that Sir Ronnie Flanagan had made reference to her as 'an immoral woman'. He added that he had never seen any evidence that she was a member of the Provisional IRA or a threat to Northern Ireland security. He also said that he had faith in the RUC threat assessment of Rosemary.

On the next day, an anonymous witness was called who held the post of Head of the Intelligence Management Group. The witness said that no intelligence had crossed his desk pointing to Rosemary's life being in danger. When he was cross-examined, the witness called Rosemary Nelson 'a terrorist' and that he had had intelligence that she allegedly passed information to the Provisional IRA about RUC investigations (gathered in the course of her job) and that the Provisional IRA had then allegedly used these details in operations. Although he believed this intelligence about Rosemary, he also thought that any criminal investigation into her was a waste of resources.

The witness also expressed his surprise that Rosemary Nelson's murder had been claimed by the Red Hand Defenders, as the LVF rarely used bombs and had little experience of such devices and shot their targets instead. This was so out of character for the LVF that the possibility that breakaway Republicans were involved in her murder had also been investigated. Although he had a low opinion of Rosemary Nelson, he told the hearing that he had regret that her murder had not been prevented.

The next witness that day was also anonymous for obvious reasons. He was an agent handler for Special Branch in Antrim. He explained to the inquiry how Loyalist paramilitaries operated, calling them 'recreational terrorists' as they often used their paramilitary status as a front for criminal activities. He added that the LVF was one of the most extreme Loyalist paramilitary groups. Like the previous witness, he was surprised that the Red Hand Defenders had claimed responsibility for Rosemary Nelson's murder, as he did not think that the LVF was able to make a bomb, in particular an Under Booby Trap Device (UBTD), such as the one used on Rosemary's car. He added that he had never seen any evidence to prove the allegations made against Rosemary.

Next, the counsel for the police, Mr Griffin, made an application to be able to participate in the closed hearing (no legal representatives present) of another anonymous witness, but no decision was immediately given. On Day 80, the closed hearing of a witness took place. It is thought that he spoke about how two leading members of the LVF, one a bomb-maker, were able to build the bomb in Belfast that killed Rosemary Nelson in Lurgan, and how they transported it there.

The following day's hearing opened with evidence from Walter Lindsay, the Principal Private Secretary (PPS) at the NIO (1996–8). Inquiry Counsel made reference to the fact that Mo Mowlam valued him and that he 'had the ear of the Minister'. Asked directly why Rosemary Nelson was not given protection in the light of the threats and alleged threats made against her, Lindsay stated that she had not met the criteria for protection. Lindsay was extremely diplomatic in his replies when asked about his own opinion of this decision, so much so that he gave no real answer either way that could be discerned.

The next witness was Nick Perry, Head of Security and

Policy Operations from 1994 to 1998, when he became PPS to Mo Mowlam and, as such, attended Security Policy meetings. Perry said that he had not known of the allegations made against Rosemary Nelson, and that he had received intelligence reports stating that Rosemary was not at high risk.

Day 82 of the RNI hearings brought the testimony of an anonymous witness, who had been an RUC uniform officer, before rising to the rank of Detective Inspector in Special Branch. He had had years of experience of working in Lurgan, Portadown and Craigavon, key areas for the inquiry. The witness explained procedures, and said that people were always informed if there was thought to be a threat to their life. Then he went into the leadership of the LVF, under Billy Wright, Mark 'Swinger' Fulton and then Fulton's younger brother who succeeded him as leader. He added that he had never seen but had knowledge of intelligence that had said that the LVF had had access to a Belfast bomb-maker before Rosemary's murder. He also spoke about the GRRC, saying that, as time passed, it began to attract Republican elements and a more 'sinister influence'. He also stated that Rosemary Nelson's collecting of GRRC complaints against the RUC to take to the European courts had put pressure on the British and Irish Governments in relation to the controversial parade disputes.

The witness was then asked questions regarding a June 1997 intelligence document. The author of the document was unknown, but it said that Rosemary Nelson had 'firm para [military] sympathies'. Reference was also made to a 31 July 1997 intelligence assessment of Joe Duffy, a senior member of the GRRC (the witness was involved in this assessment), which stated that Joe Duffy was a serious target for Loyalist paramilitaries. The witness said that he had concluded this in spite of there being no security intelligence on RUC databases saying this. He added that Rosemary Nelson's work with the GRRC on its own would have made her a potential target. Then evidence was shown to the witness relating to an application to have Rosemary Nelson's office tapped, but the witness said that he had no knowledge of this. The witness was then informed that he might be required to return to the hearings to give evidence in a closed session.

The hearings reconvened after the weekend, and another anonymous Lurgan Special Branch witness was heard. The witness stated that three separate files would have been kept on Rosemary: a source file, a target file and a personal file. He also stated that a threat assessment on Rosemary Nelson had been triggered because of intelligence that alleged that she had passed details about the police on to members of the IRA. The witness admitted that the intelligence he had read on Rosemary Nelson had led him to change his view, no longer seeing her as 'just a solicitor' going about her professional duties, but that he did not agree with the allegation that she was a terrorist. When asked about the alleged affair between Rosemary and her client Colin Duffy, his view was that their relationship had been founded on alleged meetings between the two in a Loyalist area, and that, in the witness's opinion, Colin Duffy 'had loads of affairs'.

Regarding whether there could have been a leak of intelligence about Rosemary Nelson, the witness said that he had no knowledge of such a leak, but that he could not be totally certain that a leak had not happened. Furthermore, he said that if it had, Colin Duffy would have been the primary target for violence and not Rosemary Nelson. On the Red Hand Defenders, he said that he knew of no members of that front group from Lurgan, but he was of the opinion that Loyalists had committed Rosemary Nelson's murder.

On the following day, 2 December 2008, the *Belfast Telegraph* carried a piece about allegations made in the previous day's hearing, namely the allegations that Rosemary Nelson had passed confidential information to the IRA and that she had had an affair with Colin Duffy. However, Barra McGrory, the lawyer for the Nelson family at the RNI hearings, made the following statement: 'There is no evidential basis for this belief which is apparently held on the strength of unnamed and unidentified sources, who, for all we know, could have been from the Loyalist community, who were deliberately spreading these malicious rumours about Rosemary Nelson.'

Day 85 saw evidence from another anonymous witness, another member of Special Branch, who alleged that Rosemary Nelson had created false alibis for members of the Provisional IRA and also allegedly passed on confidential information about RUC officers to them, although he also did not view her as a terrorist. However, he disagreed with his colleague who had given evidence on Day 83 that there would have been separate intelligence files on Rosemary Nelson. He said that intelligence on her would just have been kept in a file relating to Colin Duffy, suspected of allegedly being a member of the Provisional IRA in Lurgan, due to the alleged personal connection between them.

A second witness that day told the hearing that Rosemary was responsible for getting Colin Duffy off for a number of alleged IRA operations, including murders.

The following day's hearing included a former Lurgan school headmaster who knew Rosemary Nelson well. He said that there was more military activity in Lurgan than normal on the night before Rosemary's murder, and that all vehicles coming in and going out of the area were being checked at checkpoints, one of which he remembered was almost opposite Rosemary Nelson's front door. A second witness from Lurgan agreed with this, saying that that checkpoint (which they saw between 7.00 and 8.00pm on that Sunday evening) was just 30 yards from the Nelson family home.

An ex-RIR soldier was the final witness that day. He had been on checkpoints in Lurgan on the night before Rosemary's murder. When questioned, he said that he had thought that Rosemary Nelson's facial disfigurement was the result of an accident when she had allegedly thrown a petrol bomb as a teenager, and that a uniformed RUC constable had told him this, although he now knew it was wrong. The ex-soldier said that, in his opinion, lawyers who represented suspected or convicted terrorists were no better than their clients, and that he thought of such lawyers as the enemy. He had earlier made a statement to the inquiry which said, 'Mrs Nelson made herself part of the war... and unfortunately paid the price for it.' When Counsel read this back to him, he stated that he stood by what he had said. Counsel also brought to the attention of the hearing an allegation that the witness had threatened Rosemary Nelson on 29 October 1997, allegedly whispering to her, 'You know what we have got in store for you.' The ex-soldier denied this allegation, saying that he had no memory of it.

On Day 87, the hearings heard from Stephen Leach, the Associate-Director of Security and Policing (1996–2000). He went into the details about the applications of members of the GRRC under the KPPS covered much earlier in the hearings. But Leach said that he had recommended that, although the applications in question were only assessed at Level 4 risk, they should be admitted to the programme, but that the Head of the Police Division had vetoed this. When Counsel asked him if Rosemary Nelson would have received a KPPS place if she had applied personally, Leach would not be drawn on it.

On 9 December 2008, the inquiry hearings listened to Mr Jopling, a soldier who had worked as a 'spotter' (spotting people of interest during army patrols) for the Military Police and was active in Lurgan and Portadown in March 1999. Jopling said that he had been told by members of the RIR that Rosemary Nelson worked for 'them', which he took to mean Catholics suspected of terrorist offences. He was also at the scene in the aftermath of Rosemary Nelson's murder and spotted two men known to be strong Loyalists in the Nationalist area of Lurgan where Rosemary lived. When questioned why they were there, the men said that they had been visiting a Catholic graveyard, which is situated 0.2 miles from where Rosemary lived.

However, the men were not asked any more questions and their car was not searched. Jopling told the hearing that this surprised him, and he passed this 'spotting' information on to the commander of the RIR unit he was attached to, as well as filing a report on it the next day. But his commander did not do anything with the information and did not report it further. Jopling said that he had heard that this commander was particularly abusive to Catholics, more so than other RIR soldiers. This was supported at the hearing by a report focusing on this commander's failure in passing on intelligence on Loyalist paramilitary groups.

This RIR commander gave evidence anonymously after Jopling. He said that he was not prejudiced towards any paramilitary group or their causes. He added that he always asked Royal Military Police officers such as Jopling to hand in a paper report at the end of the day, but that Jopling had not done so that day.

The last anonymous witness that day knew Rosemary Nelson through having a relationship with a member of her office staff, and he said that RUC Special Branch officers had visited him in prison and asked him to collect information on Colin Duffy for them. He also recalled that one of the officers had allegedly said that Duffy and Rosemary were in a relationship and that watching Rosemary Nelson was the same as watching Colin Duffy.

Day 90 of the hearings heard evidence from a Portadown Special Branch sergeant who said that Special Branch had driven past Rosemary Nelson's home on the evening before her murder. He also said that one of the officers allegedly announced over the car radio that Rosemary's car was in the driveway so she was at home. The sergeant clarified this by saying that this announcement would have been made because of the alleged perceived relationship between Rosemary and Colin Duffy.

On the next day, a Lurgan CID sergeant, Mr Carson, gave evidence. He commented that he saw Rosemary Nelson as a lawyer just going about her business, but that her association with some clients could have provoked negative views of her among some officers. He added that he had had to serve notices on two RUC officers alleged to have made remarks to Rosemary's clients to the effect that Rosemary Nelson was 'a money-grabbing bitch' and that she was 'a Provo solicitor' (Rosemary herself had made complaints about these incidents). The witness told the hearing that such remarks were possible as police interviews were not recorded then, but that he felt that the remarks were not characteristic of the particular officers involved in the complaints. He had also said in his earlier recorded statement to the inquiry that there had been a helicopter capable of making recordings in Lurgan on the day of Rosemary's murder. But, when he had told the Army to preserve the footage, they said that no footage had been recorded that day.

On Days 92 and 93 of the inquiry hearings, evidence was taken anonymously from a former Chief Superintendent in the RUC. He had taken notes at a meeting between the RUC Chief Constable Sir Ronnie Flanagan and the Assistant Chief Constable Raymond White and the UN Special Rapporteur Param Cumaraswamy, focusing on alleged threats made to Rosemary Nelson by RUC officers and lack of access to a client. The witness had noted down that Assistant Chief Constable White had made a comment about the suspicions of the Independent Commissioner for Holding

Centres Sir Louis Blom-Cooper regarding some solicitors possibly working for paramilitaries. It might be remembered that, much earlier in the RNI hearings, Blom-Cooper himself had given evidence stating that he did not hold this view. It transpired that the witness's notes were different from those taken by Param Cumaraswamy's UN assistant, Mr Parra, and this misunderstanding had never been resolved. The witness also said that the subject of Pat Finucane came up in the meeting, probably in relation to the safety of lawyers. The witness also said that the RUC kept a file on 'issues involving Rosemary Nelson'.

After that, the former Assistant Chief Constable of the RUC Raymond White appeared at the hearing and said that he was of the opinion that complaints were made by paramilitaries in order to hinder RUC criminal investigations. White confirmed that it was either himself or Sir Ronnie Flanagan who had made the comment about some solicitors possibly working for paramilitaries at the meeting with the UN Special Rapporteur.

On 17 December 2008, Day 94, an ex-Chief Superintendent in the RUC Special Branch gave his evidence anonymously. Under questioning, it was inferred that Special Branch were critical of the Nelson murder investigation led by Colin Port, in that they felt that the CID should have been investigated and not their department. But the witness said that he himself had never seen any tensions between Special Branch and the CID, although evidence showed that there was a lack of trust in Special Branch because it thought that the CID and the Port investigation team had tapped their phones. It also came out that an application *had* been made to carry out surveillance on a house owned by Rosemary Nelson, and the witness made clear that there was an alleged leading terrorist living there. Earlier testimony in the hearings leaves us in no doubt about to whom this refers.

The ex-Chief Superintendent said that he was not surprised by accusations of alleged collusion between RUC officers and the people who murdered Rosemary Nelson, and that in his view it was a strategy used by alleged terrorists to smear the RUC. In the final revelation of the day, it emerged that a March 1999 intelligence document stated that the UFF were worried that they could not account for one of their bombs and that it might have been the one used to kill Rosemary Nelson. Counsel pointed out that some high-level managers had stated to the inquiry that they had never received this intelligence.

On Day 95, an anonymous witness who had served in the UDR and then the RIR was called. He gave evidence in relation to the enhanced security activity in the vicinity of Rosemary Nelson's Lurgan home on the evening before her murder – Sunday, 14 March 1999. He said that he was involved in two helicopter surveillance sorties that evening, surveying the nearby Kilwilkie Estate and flying over Rosemary's home a few times in the process. However, as the hearing heard, the visual flight recordings of the first sortie seemed to have gone missing, but there was no explanation offered as to why.

A further anonymous witness, who had been an Operations Officer in the RIR in 1999, gave evidence the following day. He referred to a security alert around Kilwilkie on 14 March 1999, regarding a suspect device that had been reported by a detective at Lurgan RUC station. However, local residents disposed of the device on some waste ground and a search was not carried out until the next day.

The former RUC Chief Constable Sir Ronnie Flanagan gave evidence to the RNI hearings for three consecutive days, Days 98–100. Flanagan was Chief Constable from 1996 until the RUC was wound down in 2001, although he effectively remained in control until he resigned and handed over the reins to the PSNI in 2002. An earlier witness had commented that he took a more hands-on approach to the job than his predecessor. On Day 98, Flanagan started to give his evidence. Rory Phillips QC, Leading Counsel for the Inquiry, questioned Flanagan, beginning with the disputed fact of whether there had been an RUC Special Branch file kept on Rosemary Nelson prior to her murder.

As we know, more than one witness (in fact, the whole transcripts reveal many) had testified that there would have been such a file, as it was automatic procedure if an Special Branch 'number' had been given to a person, and Phillips said that such an allocation had been made. However, Flanagan confirmed his previous assertion in his answers – he had no knowledge 'of any files, paper or otherwise' on Rosemary Nelson. Flanagan also spoke about the operating styles of respective Secretaries of State under whom he had been Chief Constable – he said that Sir Patrick Mayhew had allowed the RUC to be more operationally independent than his successor, Dr Mo Mowlam.

Then an April 1997 letter from a US Senator to the British Ambassador to the United States was shown to the hearing. It contained the allegation that Rosemary Nelson had received death threats through her clients being questioned at Gough Barracks detention centre, allegedly by RUC officers. Flanagan's response was that he had had no knowledge of the letter and, if he had, he would have ensured that a full investigation was carried out into the allegation. Next, a letter from Amnesty International, expressing similar concerns on Rosemary's behalf, was referred to. Flanagan said that he had no recollection of that particular letter either, although it was the type of letter that would have crossed his desk when he was Chief Constable. He also remarked that, in his opinion, BIRW, which also looked out for Rosemary Nelson, was not balanced in its view (this supported his earlier recorded statement to the inquiry).

Regarding the meeting with UN Special Rapporteur Param Cumaraswamy and the contentious issue of who made the comment about some Northern Ireland defence lawyers perhaps working for paramilitaries, Flanagan denied that he had said it. He had asked the Special Rapporteur to have the report amended as the remark had been wrongly attributed to him.

Next on the agenda was the RUC threat assessment on Rosemary Nelson and the level of Flanagan's involvement in it. The NIO had set the assessment in motion, and Flanagan said that it was not usual for the Chief Constable to become directly involved in individual threat assessments. However, Flanagan thought he had been involved in Rosemary's threat assessment (the only case he had done this for) because he had been asked for advice by the Chief Superintendent in charge of the assessment.

A handwritten note on the Rosemary Nelson threat assessment report was then read out to the hearing. It stated that, after a discussion with Flanagan and another person, there was nothing more that the RUC could do for Rosemary at that time. Flanagan was questioned as to why this conclusion was reached. He said that it was possibly because it was known that if RUC officers visited Rosemary at her home or office it would have caused her anxiety, and that local police were the best people to keep an eye on her. He added that it had been the NIO's responsibility to decide if Rosemary was suitable for the KPPS, and was not within the RUC's remit.

Then the focus turned to comments that it was alleged Flanagan had made in a meeting with a representative of the ICPC and a senior NIO official. The alleged comment made reference to the rumours of an alleged affair between Rosemary Nelson and Colin Duffy. Flanagan denied that he would have made the comment in the meeting, but he might have said it privately to the NIO official.

The final day of Flanagan's evidence began with reference to the *Man Without a Future* pamphlet (which did the rounds in Drumcree in 1998 and alleged that Rosemary was a former bomber and giving her personal details). Also, there was the note that made a direct and sinister threat to her. Flanagan told the hearing that the pamphlet would not have affected the threat assessments on Rosemary carried out in April and August/September 1998, as it was plainly propaganda. He said that the threat note was more serious, and could have been analysed for DNA but that, in his experience, he had never known a terrorist group write a threat note to someone whom they 'had already identified as a target'. The hearing was then told that, although Paul Mageean of the CAJ had sent the threat note to the NIO along with the pamphlet, Flanagan had not seen the threat note until after Rosemary Nelson's murder. Flanagan also said that the second Nelson threat assessment conducted in August/September 1998 had not been his idea or directed by him.

Then Operation Indus was discussed, which was an application to put a listening device into the house owned by Rosemary and leased to an alleged 'leading Republican' (Colin Duffy). Counsel said that the evidence seen by the inquiry pointed to the application having not been given the go-ahead. Phillips added that the 'leading Republican' had been to Rosemary's office on occasions, and Flanagan said that he had not known about this. He also said that he would not have thought that Indus would be approved, as Rosemary would have had legal privileges as a lawyer that prevented this.

Flanagan's evidence concluded on the subject of the state of relations between Colin Port's team and RUC Special Branch during the Nelson murder investigation. Flanagan said that he had no knowledge of a major problem in relations, but there had been 'rubbing points' (moments of friction).

That same day, the RNI hearings heard from Sir David Phillips, Chief Constable of Kent, who at the very earliest stage had advised on the Nelson murder investigation.

Significantly, during this testimony, Counsel referred to the fact that Sam Kincaid, Senior Investigating Officer on the murder investigation, had recommended that the RUC officers against whom Rosemary Nelson had made allegations should play no role in the investigation of her murder.

On Day 102 of the hearings, an intelligence document was seen as evidence and stated that, allegedly, an army patrol had stopped Rosemary Nelson's car at a checkpoint once and that Colin Duffy was inside it. A further document alleged that, on a different occasion, both Rosemary and Duffy had been stopped by a patrol in a different car, and that Rosemary had said that the stop was interrupting a meeting in progress with Duffy, her client. Another document (thought to be dated February 1999, the month before Rosemary's murder) referred to Loyalist paramilitaries and stated that the Red Hand Defenders and the Orange Volunteers were about to escalate their attacks against Catholics over a period of 12 days.

There was an adjournment of the hearings from 23 January until 9 February 2009, when they reconvened on Day 103. A member of the Security Service who had been involved in the Nelson murder investigation gave evidence anonymously from behind a screen and without a legal representative. The witness said that he had heard some concerns from RUC Special Branch officers at the time regarding the progress and direction of the investigation, headed by Colin Port. The concerns were that the team were not familiar enough with Northern Ireland and that the team's approach to gathering evidence was conducive to short-term goals (for the investigation), but could jeopardise long-term operations. The witness added that he agreed that there was friction between the investigation team, Special

Branch and CID, and that Colin Port's view that his team 'actively' had to request information (instead of being offered it, presumably) was correct.

On the following day, after a witness was heard in closed session for an hour, the witness was then heard openly at the hearing. It can be gleaned from the questioning that the witness was an officer in a division of MI5 involved in counter-terrorism. Counsel referred to intelligence which alleged that the Orange Volunteers, a prominent Loyalist group, was identifying targets with the help of the security services. The witness said that he did not see how this was relevant to Colin Port's investigation, and, if Port wanted further explanation of the intelligence, he would officially have to make representations.

Day 105, 11 February 2009, opened with Counsel outlining the next focus of the hearings, the examination of the Nelson murder investigation. After the parameters of the examination were laid out, the hearing heard from Sam Kincaid, who had been a Detective Superintendent in 1998 and acted as the Senior Investigating Officer on the Nelson murder investigation, and whose evidence would continue into the next day.

Kincaid referred to the co-operation (or lack of it) between RUC Special Branch and CID being a problem, especially about Operation Shubr (outlined earlier) which he had not even been aware of. An intelligence document was then used in evidence, and it mentioned a meeting between a Mid-Ulster Loyalist and a member of the paramilitary organisation the UFF. It may be remembered from earlier in the hearings that the UFF had been concerned because one of their bombs (similar to the one that killed Rosemary) had gone missing before her murder. The intelligence document also included this information. Kincaid said that he did not want to discuss this issue in open session.

Kincaid went on to give his opinion that he thought that Mid-Ulster Loyalists were not capable of building the bomb that killed Rosemary, but that they had the capability of planting it. It might be recalled that earlier in the hearings we heard that the LVF allegedly had access to a bomb-maker in Belfast.

The next two days saw evidence being given by Kincaid's Deputy Investigating Officer on the murder investigation, who remained anonymous and behind a screen. An intelligence document was referred to which alleged that Rosemary Nelson had known that her client Colin Duffy had allegedly killed Kevin Conway on 17 February 1998. Conway had been seized in his Lurgan home by armed men and his body was found two days later a few miles away. The RUC had taken the view at the time that Republican paramilitaries committed the murder. Both Counsel and an Inquiry Panel Member asked the witness if Rosemary Nelson would have been in danger if this alleged piece of intelligence were true. The witness said that first, in his opinion, the Provisional IRA would not have murdered a lawyer (obviously to silence her about what she knew). He added that it would have been Colin Duffy who was in danger from the Provisional IRA if he had allegedly told his lawyer about his alleged involvement.

Attention then turned to the bomb attached to Rosemary Nelson's car. We saw earlier in this book that the magnets used in the bomb were thought to have gone missing from the Harland & Wolff Shipyard in Belfast. A forensic scientist had given his opinion that it could not be proven that the magnets came from that source, although questioning brought out that there were visible paint marks on the bomb material, like those used on magnets at the shipyard. He had also said that the bomb evidence he had examined was unlikely to have been of 'Republican origin', going some way to dispel the theory that Republican paramilitaries had committed the murder, despite the Loyalist Red Hand Defenders claiming it.

The next day, Day 108, another scientist disagreed with the first, as the former had found that the bomb looked similar to ones used by the Loyalist UDA and the second did not to the same extent. However, a further witness, Mr Provost, an English policeman and a member of the Port murder investigation team, discussed the two different scientific opinions, but it was said that, overall, both scientists had concluded that it was a Loyalist device.

On 19–20 February 2009, Days 110 and 111, evidence came from a very senior member of RUC Special Branch who remained anonymous. Rory Phillips QC referred to the intelligence report entered into evidence a few days before which alleged that members of the security services were helping the Orange Volunteers to identify potential targets. The witness responded that this was not relevant to the Rosemary Nelson case, as the Orange Volunteers did not have a strong base in the area where she had lived. When pressed, he said, 'We had clear arrangements with Mr Port that, if anything of that nature emerged in relation to security services allegedly outside of the Nelson case, that that would be investigated separately. I'm aware of that having been done and that's a matter of record.'

The witness was further questioned about intelligence that could perhaps indicate alleged collusion between the security services and Loyalist paramilitaries. The witness said that the April 2000 document referring to the Orange Volunteers (made after Rosemary's murder) would have been given over to Port's team if it was 'in any way connected or relevant'.

On Day 112, 23 February 2009, a former Special Branch Inspector testified anonymously. Counsel made reference to an intelligence document that alleged that a leading member of the Provisional IRA and Rosemary Nelson had been attempting to create a false alibi for the latter's client, Colin Duffy. This was in relation to his arrest for the murder of the UDR soldier John Lyness, covered earlier. The witness said that, in his opinion, Rosemary would not have created the alibi actively by choice, but that he thought that Rosemary would have known that the Provisional IRA member was creating it. This allegation has never been proved or substantiated.

Also that day, the ex-leader of the LVF, Mark 'Swinger' Fulton, who had masterminded Rosemary Nelson's murder and later committed suicide in prison, was referred to. In the same document that contained the allegation about the alleged alibi, there was intelligence that stated that Fulton had claimed that his group had bomb-making capabilities. This was allegedly in relation to contacts that Fulton had in the RIR and the RUC. When questioned, the witness made reference to an RIR soldier allegedly connected with Loyalist paramilitaries who was arrested after Rosemary's murder. The witness said that it was impossible to say if this was the contact that Fulton had referred to, and he couldn't be certain that Fulton had not had a contact within the RUC.

There was a further 18 days of hearings, but the key evidence is outlined above.

After 130 days of examination, the RNI hearings came to an end, and the Inquiry Panel retired to formulate the report that is still pending.

The Billy Wright Inquiry has now reported, as we have seen, finding only negligence. The Robert Hamill Inquiry is still under way, but no inquiry has been announced into Patrick Finucane's murder, more than 20 years after his killing.

10

THE NEED FOR TRUTH

In all the facts and legal complexities surrounding the murder of Rosemary Nelson, it should not be forgotten that she was a human being, much loved by her family and close friends. She left behind a husband and three young children who are now adults. Rosemary Nelson must not be seen as a mere pawn in the convoluted and dangerous world of Northern Ireland politics. She was a woman cruelly murdered in her prime at the age of 40.

As her sister Caitlin said in an interview with the *Irish News* on 13 March 2003, almost exactly four years after Rosemary's murder, 'We never wanted anyone to use Rosemary's name for their own ends. We did not want this to become a green [Republican] issue. It's a justice issue.'

Her brother Eunan, speaking in the middle of Rosemary's murder investigation (thought at that point to have cost £7m), and after Colin Port had withdrawn from it, said, 'But the investigation has polarised political opinion. What do Unionists see? They see X amount of pounds poured into an investigation that has got us nowhere.' He added, 'We feel let down. Very let down.'

Rosemary's sister, Bernie, added, 'Rosemary, who believed in justice, deserves justice herself. That is the bottom line. If it had been one of us, our Rosemary would have left no stone unturned.'

Although, as we have seen, there had been arrests for Rosemary Nelson's murder, by late 2010 nobody has ever been charged with her murder, even though Sir Ronnie Flanagan said in early 2009 that the names of her killers were known to the RUC soon after her murder. While mounting enough evidence to convict is very difficult, and the DPP will only authorise a prosecution if there is a reasonable chance of conviction, it is easy to understand why Rosemary Nelson's family feel very disappointed – particularly because of the alleged State collusion question hanging over Rosemary's murder. The RNI may have given the family more optimism, but the results of the inquiry are what matters.

But Rosemary is remembered with love, pride and much affection. Her sister Bernie said, 'Every Christmas since Rosemary died, there are women who have given my mother remembrance cards. And they are always just signed, "To Rosemary." You know what, we don't even know what Rosemary did for them.'

On 19 February 2009, on the twentieth anniversary of his murder, there was an international conference held in Dublin in tribute to Patrick Finucane's life and work. The conference heard that the British Government had implied that it might not even hold a 'controlled' inquiry into Finucane's murder, although it was still considering recommendations.

As the Pat Finucane Centre's resources show, Pat Finucane's son John said in response that the British Government 'appears to be preparing to break promises that they made, not only to ourselves, but also to the Irish Government and others. The question needs to be asked: just in whose interest would it be not to have an inquiry into my father's murder?' Also present at the conference were Finucane's widow Geraldine, Jane Winter of BIRW, Michael Mansfield QC and the former UN Special Rapporteur Param Cumaraswamy.

Michael Mansfield QC was horrified that the British Government was suggesting that holding a public inquiry into Pat Finucane's murder would not be in the public interest. Mansfield said, 'The only ones who should decide what's in the public interest are the public.' He added, 'It is not just because Pat's family deserves to know the extent of [alleged] collusion – as do so many families – but because there will be no genuine, lasting peace in Ireland until there is justice... justice must be built upon the full disclosure of the truth.'

Param Cumaraswamy said, 'I was given an assurance by Tony Blair in April 2001 that there would be an independent inquiry into Pat's murder, which, eight years on, has not eventuated.' Cumaraswamy also spoke about the failure of the British Government, the RUC and the Law Society of Northern Ireland to give protection to Rosemary Nelson.

The fact that Loyalists were seen in the vicinity of where Rosemary Nelson was killed on that very day and were questioned is potentially very enlightening. Why was this sighting and preliminary questioning not followed up by the Army or the RUC? The answer to that question will probably never be publicly known, but it certainly breeds cynicism, and also leads to the pessimistic but realistic conclusion that nobody will ever be convicted for making the bomb and putting it under Rosemary Nelson's BMW on 14–15 March 1999. How did the terrorists get through the checkpoints, especially as we know that they visited Rosemary's house not once but twice on that night/early morning. Why were the threats and alleged threats against Rosemary not taken more seriously, despite repeated pleas from the US Congress, the UN, Amnesty International and many other NGOs and prominent people? How could these threats be investigated thoroughly, when many of them are said to have been made by RUC officers and the RUC was investigating and assessing these allegations?

Regarding the allegations made about Rosemary Nelson, was she associated with Republican paramilitaries as alleged? Did she have that alleged relationship with her client, Colin Duffy, now in prison, and had they collaborated in the murder of British soldiers? Did she help to give Duffy false alibis as alleged? Did Rosemary pass confidential police information to the Provisional IRA? These allegations are all unsubstantiated, but in getting to the truth they must be considered to give fair balance, as, if any one of them were true, Rosemary Nelson would have been considered a legitimate paramilitary target, as an associate of paramilitaries or even an alleged member.

The question of whether or not there was State collusion overshadows the whole Rosemary Nelson case. As said in the introduction, it is known that the British security services were involved with Loyalist paramilitaries, as the IRA and other Republican paramilitaries were seen as the common enemy. As Richard Belfield asserts in his book *The Secret History of Assassination*, 'The British... worked closely with the various Protestant terrorist organisations, particularly the Ulster Volunteer Force, providing them with intelligence, information, explosives and weapons.'

Northern Ireland is a more peaceful place now than it was in 1999 when Rosemary Nelson was murdered. The breakthrough of the Good Friday Agreement (the year before Rosemary's killing) has ensured an end to large-scale atrocities. But there have been many murders since Rosemary was killed and some of them have been covered in this book. As late as 6 September 2010, a little boy at a mainly Catholic school in Antrim picked up a pipe bomb he found on the ground and took it into school. The school was evacuated. The type of bomb (which has killed in the past) has long been 'a favourite' with Loyalists, and indeed a Loyalist paramilitary splinter group claimed responsibility for it. What was the motive for leaving the bomb lying around? Obviously to stir up sectarian tensions and break the fragile 'peace'.

If there was State collusion in the execution of Rosemary Nelson's murder, then it was systematic and not an isolated incident. Why did Judge Cory conclude that there was the possibility of alleged State collusion in Pat Finucane's murder in 1989? How did the Loyalists know that Sam Marshall would be leaving Lurgan RUC station at a certain time before murdering him in 1990? Why did RUC officers sit watching in their Land Rover in Portadown in 1996, as a Loyalist mob beat Robert Hamill to death? How did the INLA get the guns into prison to kill Billy Wright in 1997? All of these questions and many more need answering and, if there has been systematic collusion, that would be very frightening.

Northern Ireland was just emerging from the Troubles when Rosemary Nelson was murdered. Many considered the situation there as a civil war during that period and after. Did institutions such as the RUC, Security Service and the Army, under the aegis of the British Government, feel that there were no rules and that winning that war was all that mattered? Were the 'high' standards of British democracy not met in practice? Some of the incidents described in this book are deeply shocking to anyone who lives on the British mainland, although the victims here were also British subjects. The first rule of a government is to protect all the citizens in its care. If the allegations of collusion in Rosemary Nelson's murder were ever proven to be true, the British Government and by proxy every British citizen would have blood on their hands.

The truth about who really killed Rosemary Nelson needs to come out and justice needs to be done. The RNI hearings threw up many interesting points. Leading Counsel for the Inquiry Rory Phillips QC said in his closing speech regarding the RUC that its attitude was 'all of a piece' and that it had regarded Rosemary Nelson as 'someone over whom it would not be worth taking any great trouble'. Why? Former leader of the Nelson murder investigation team Colin Port told the inquiry that working with the RUC to gather evidence was like 'wading through treacle while treading on eggshells'. Why?

So, who killed Rosemary Nelson? Well, although we know that the LVF under Mark 'Swinger' Fulton was behind her murder, we do not know the names of the person who built the bomb and those who planted it. However, Fulton is as guilty as anybody else, as he masterminded Rosemary's murder, but he killed himself in prison in 2002, a broken and paranoid man, so there will never be a confession or punishment. We also know that, if the State was in some way involved, whether actively or negligently, there will be no confession and probably no punishment. But we await the findings of the RNI and hope that it is not a whitewash.

Rosemary Nelson was a woman of intelligence and tenacity, who, in her role as lawyer, worked very hard and effectively for her clients, sometimes beyond the call of duty. It was her skilled representation of her clients which was the main cause for her becoming an object of resentment – and, for some, hatred – among the various factions of her own splintered community. She was forthright about the alleged abuses and threats she suffered, particularly in regard to the allegations raised by some of her clients against certain officers within the RUC. Ironically, giving these allegations, wide publicity was exactly what she felt would protect her. Why did she continue on this path, when there are claims that she was receiving threats, verbal and written, on a regular basis, some of them said to be venal and absolutely terrifying?

We know that she liked to keep up a brave, carefree front, but that she occasionally confided her fears to those closest to her. She was only human like the rest of us, after all. She was a fighter, who refused to be silenced while alive, but perhaps a level of crusading came into play in her fight. She had rapidly become a revered figurehead for a cause, highly respected in her own community. Such crusades are dangerous, and Rosemary

Nelson paid the highest price for it, but we will never know how much internal and external pressure she felt to continue, or whether it was her own heart that drove her on. Those closest to her were extremely concerned for her and warned her to lower her profile, or at least to be more careful in her movements and actions.

There is also evidence to show that in the last months of her life she was trying to spend more time with her family and lead a more balanced life. But perhaps it was too late, and she had already been marked as a target for some time. The year 1997 was the turning point, according to the evidence, when Rosemary Nelson truly became prominent and began making media appearances, and was soon seen as a significant figure in Northern Ireland, especially in Armagh. Was her card marked from that time, as Billy Wright's diary showed, and, after Wright had been murdered, were his wishes carried out by Mark 'Swinger' Fulton?

LP Hartley famously wrote in *The Go-Between*, 'The past is a foreign country; they do things differently there.' That is, of course, true, but should we not learn from the past to improve our future, especially as the deep roots of rumour and suspicion concerning the State's role in Northern Ireland are possibly still in place? To truly leave the past behind, the people of Northern Ireland, from both sides of the political/religious divide, need to feel real trust in the systems that protect and serve them.

On the twentieth anniversary of Patrick Finucane's murder, his widow Geraldine eloquently said that 'the society that forgets its past, or, worse, tries to pretend it never existed, is doomed to repeat it'. That is why the truth of who killed both Patrick Finucane and Rosemary Nelson needs to come to light. To move on, mistakes or terrible actions have to be admitted. As the great Irish-American writer F Scott Fitzgerald wrote at the end of *The Great Gatsby*: 'So we beat on, boats against the current, borne back ceaselessly into the past.'

Until everyone who was involved in Rosemary Nelson's murder – however insignificant or decisive their action, whether active or negligent – is brought to justice, those currents of the past will continue to pull Northern Ireland back to the darkness of the Troubles.